# DEATH

## AT

# CROSS

# PLAINS

# DEATH
## AT
# CROSS
# PLAINS

## AN ALABAMA
## RECONSTRUCTION
## TRAGEDY

GENE L. HOWARD

*With a Foreword by Gary B. Mills*

**THE UNIVERSITY OF ALABAMA PRESS**
*Tuscaloosa and London*

**Library of Congress Cataloging in Publication Data**

Howard, Gene L., 1940–
  Death at Cross Plains.

  Bibliography: p.
  Includes index.
  1. Reconstruction—Alabama—Cross Plains. 2. Cross
Plains (Ala.)—Race relations. 3. Lynching—Alabama—
Cross Plains—History—19th century. 4. Luke,
William C., d. 1870. 5. Missionaries—Alabama—Cross
Plains—Biography. 6. Civil rights workers—Alabama—
Cross Plains—Biography. 7. Cross Plains (Ala.)—
Biography. I. Title.
F334.C68H68    1984        364.1′523′0976163        83-5839

ISBN 0-8173-0749-4

First Paperback Edition 1994

1  2  3  4  /  99  98  97  96  95  94

TO:

William J. Calvert; a gentleman
and a friend.

# CONTENTS

# ACKNOWLEDGMENTS

My experience with the Cross Plains story began in late 1978, when Lane Weatherbee, editor of the Piedmont *Independent-Journal*, shared several articles with me about a mass hanging that was part of the city's history. He obtained much of his information from county historian Jack Boozer, and serialized an account of the tragedy for his readers.

The articles intrigued me as I recognized several universal themes in the story of old Cross Plains. I became curious about William Luke and why he became the center of controversy so far removed from his native Canada, and why Patona never experienced the industrial growth that would have made the town a thriving metropolis. The answer to these questions is this work, essentially an interpretive synthesis of several years of historical research.

I am grateful to Dr. Grace Gates, author and historian, whose editorial advice contributed to the success of the study.

As we remember again what others seem so willing to forget, the justification for our recollections—if we need one—can be framed by a line from William Faulkner's novel, *Intruder in the Dust:* "The past is never dead. It is not even past."

GENE HOWARD

# FOREWORD

The political, social, and economic turmoil that gripped the South after the Civil War created an atmosphere conducive to violence amid a people already fiercely proud and exceedingly passionate. The federal Reconstruction of the defeated Confederacy closed to southerners those avenues of protest against injustice that are customary in civilized society, forcing them to seek both defense and vengeance by more surreptitious means, against whatever targets might be accessible. The subjected southerners could do nothing to reach the roots of the very real problems caused by a lost war and a ruined economy, but they could—and did—strike at the people who contributed to their plight; and amid their frustration, it seldom mattered whether their victims were actually guilty or merely symbolic.

Traditionally, history has tended to relate all violence during this era to organizations such as the Ku Klux Klan and to portray the victims as innocent idealists. In reality, there can be no doubt that some of the deaths and assaults were unrelated to politics. Personal vengeance and satisfaction for affronts to honor were important tenets of the code inherited by generations of southerners. Such individual expressions of violence continued to occur during Reconstruction, and many victims of this era were by no means innocent. Some had fomented violence or had purposefully acted in a provocative manner.

The newly potent groups within southern society—the carpetbaggers, scalawags, and blacks—were a myriad assortment, motivated by diverse factors. To view them all as righteous idealists intent upon creating a utopia in the South is both naive and indefensible. The southern-born scalawag certainly was aware of the nature of his own people, he presumably calculated his personal risk, and he could hardly have been surprised at the South's response to the problems of Reconstruction. The carpetbagger, alien to the southern culture, displayed little tolerance for the values he did not understand and consequently brought wrath upon himself with ease. Finally, there were the more noble-minded, who did not fear even though they might vaguely realize the dangers of their mission. The apostles of enlightenment, spirited and zealous, did indeed exist. Beclouded by their idealism, such men saw only the good they expected their ministry to accomplish and were unresponsive to the discomfort that their narrow-minded righteousness stirred in others. Incredulity often marked such men, who ultimately confronted death in the eyes of an angry mob.

Such a man was William C. Luke, a former minister who had fallen from grace and been reborn as a missionary, committed to the goals he had set for himself in his second chance at living a spiritual life. Southerners saw him as a do-gooder in search of good to do. Ironically, in but a few months after he found his purpose, he lost his life.

Why? Fundamentally, Luke did not understand humanity as it existed in the great mission field that he chose for himself. As a Canadian, he could not empathize with the southern psyche, the anomalous state in which individuals could display abundant hospitality to strangers while their society remained impenetrable. Unexposed to the years of civil conflict, he did not comprehend the desire for vengeance that simmers in a conquered people long after their forced surrender. As a disciple of brotherly love, he could not fathom the fear that is felt by people who have simultaneously been stripped of their defenses and overwhelmed by masses of freedmen eager to assert their independence and power. In the course of southern Reconstruction untold numbers of men fell victim to misunderstanding. Luke was such a man.

Gene Howard's exhaustive research and penetrating scrutiny of the events surrounding the death of William C. Luke has failed to uncover the stereotyped carpetbagger. Luke was not the proverbial opportunist, unscrupulous and corrupt, determined to enrich himself at the expense of an unfortunate people. Neither a politician nor a Radical Republican, he was at heart a teacher. From the onset of his brief southern sojourn, his varied talents were committed to the service of unfortunates of both races. The fortitude with which he met his death was equivalent to that of any martyr.

What of the men who placed the fatal rope around the neck of Luke and his comrades-in-death? Again, stereotype pervades the historical treatment of such classes in American writings. They were uniformly callous to the feelings of humanity, their cowardice cloaked in sheets of white as if to offer a symbolic purification and exaltation of their deeds. Howard's *Death at Cross Plains* belies this stereotype. Luke's executioners emerge as forthright, though misguided, and by cultural heritage, too prone to violence. They were sincere in their concern for their society, purposeful in their quest for a solution, and passionate in its execution. Yet through the fatal climax, Luke's adversaries evidenced a peculiar respect toward their victim, for it is part of the southern character to admire a fearless and unwavering foe.

To what end were the lynchings which occurred that fateful night in 1870 at Cross Plains, Alabama? The men who executed this deed, and countless others across the South, saw the act as a clear and potent warning to those who threatened the South's traditional way of life. To their political enemies, it represented another explosive episode—even a welcomed tool—to underscore their argument that the South remained unreconstructed and that harsher measures of retribution and control should be applied. Yet political Reconstruction did end in the South, in the midst of many continued acts of rebellion; and the South has undergone far more changes than even those feared by the men of Cross Plains.

The effectiveness or the futility of the actions taken at countless crossroads of the postwar South has been one of the most unresolved questions of American history. Howard's *Death at Cross Plains* does not purport to offer the ultimate analysis of the issue. It does provide a poignant view of one critical episode in history, and it will surely serve to fuel continued debates.

GARY B. MILLS
The University of Alabama

# DEATH
## AT
# CROSS
# PLAINS

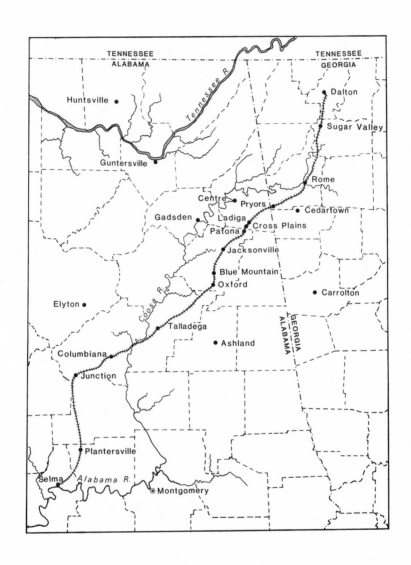

# I

# Cross Plains
# in 1870

✝ THE VILLAGE OF Cross Plains was set in the
foothills of the Appalachian Mountains, where the
plateaus diminish in northeastern Alabama and the Appalachian Valley opens into the coastal plains. The
Weisner Ridges bounded the village on the north and
south. The southern ridge was known as Duggar Mountain, twenty-one hundred feet of timber and rock adjoin-
ing Rattlesnake Mountain.[1]

The village was in the borderlands, between the
mountains and the lowland plains—between the mountain people and the cotton planters.[2]

The country was divided into natural gateways, small
ridges, rolling hills, and crossroads. Fifty inches of annual rainfall washed millions of tons of native topsoil into
the Gulf of Mexico each year. In many places around the
village, the loss of soil exposed barren, red hills.[3]

Calhoun County was surveyed from a Creek land ces-
sion. The Creeks (Muskogees) ceded the territory in
March 1832; the county was organized the following
December. The Indians that formerly occupied the land
traveled the infamous Trail of Tears to Oklahoma, leaving their natural heritage to the white man. These civi-

1

lized tribes left behind only the names of towns, streams, and other landmarks in the county.[4]

Gold was discovered along the southernmost border of the old county line in the 1830s. Arbacoochee and Chulafinnee flourished as booming gold towns until news of the California bonanza drew the adventurous miners westward.[5]

The old boundary line that divided the Cherokee Indian nation in the upland fields of northeastern Alabama from the Creeks, who had inhabited the waterways in the central part of the state, crossed the county below the village. West of Cross Plains the Choccolocco Mountains began; the most prominent elevation, Chimney Peak, rose sharply, clearly visible eleven miles from the village. Georgia was fourteen miles to the east.[6]

Jacksonville, the county seat, was built on a square atop one of the long, rolling hills so common to the area. The courthouse was in the middle of the hilltop square. Strategically located in the center of the county, Jacksonville, with 958 citizens in 1870, led the political and economic affairs of the area.[7]

Several tall-columned mansions had been built along the main roads of the town, reflecting the wealth of its leading citizens. Following the Civil War, Jacksonville was the home for many former Confederate officers. The Forney family sent five of its sons to fight in the army, two of them serving as generals. Gallant John Pelham was buried in the local cemetery after a short, heroic career as a gunnery officer.[8]

The people of Calhoun County, like most southerners, were democratic by nature. They maintained a proud independence, considering themselves equal to all other men. Eighteen hundred voted for the Democratic party in the 1870 elections while four hundred cast Republican ballots.[9]

The road between Cross Plains and Jacksonville lay through open plantation fields and unbroken pine forests. At times it paralleled the new railroad bed. During the wet season the road was little more than a width of mud in which the wheels of wagons and buggies sank halfway up to the axles. Cross Plains was a scattered and loosely organized village in 1870. The essential feature that gave it some semblance of a municipality was the intersection of two main roads that crossed, forming the heart of the community.

From the north a road from Kentucky and Tennessee passed through the village to southern Alabama and southern Georgia. From the Appalachian Valley to the northeast another important road from Knoxville and Rome crossed the northern route to Montgomery and Mobile. On the south side of the crossroads was a public well, a benevolent gesture to the travelers who plied the thoroughfares.

About the distance of a city block north of the crossroads, a railroad ran west to east through the village. The Selma, Rome, and Dalton Railroad Company had completed laying the track two years earlier, building a loading dock to accommodate freight but only a crude office for the agent and passengers. The facilities were built on private property because of the company's haste to finish the line.[10]

Across the road from the depot, a new hotel had been erected after the railroad was completed to the Georgia line. Called the Cross Plains House, it was three stories high with a broad porch, known as a gallery in the South, across the front and part of the way down the left side of the building next to the railroad tracks.[11]

Just north of these two primary structures was the only school in the village; it was named Cross Plains Institute.

3

Its advertisements promised, "Cross Plains is healthy. The society is first class, consequently all moral restraint will be thrown around the pupils." Major Andrew D. Bailey, a Confederate army veteran, headed the staff of teachers that included his younger sister, who taught music.[12]

The village had several general stores, one drugstore, two barrooms, one wagon and buggy shop, two steam cotton gins, a shoe shop, a blacksmith shop, and a Masonic lodge. Most of the more valuable property was around the crossroads. The post office was in a two-story brick building shaded by several large oaks on a corner west of the crossroads. In May 1870, railroad officials in nearby Patona had the name of the post office changed from Cross Plains to Patona, and Henry Barney was named postmaster. But in June the name was changed back, and Rufus Penny became the new postmaster.[13]

The new Methodist church, completed the previous year, was built on the public road that forked north of the village and paralleled the main road toward Nancey's Creek.[14]

The nearest river was thirty miles north of Cross Plains. It was the Coosa that came from Rome, Georgia, coursing its way through Alabama for more than three hundred miles. Two streams were nearby: the Terrapin in the Ladiga community to the east and Nancey's Creek four miles below the village. Once there was discussion around the countryside about digging a canal from the Tennessee River, which ran through Guntersville, to Gadsden, to connect the two rivers for commercial traffic. It was only fifty miles between them, but the $9 million estimated proved to be more than the state could afford.

Most of the people around Cross Plains farmed. They were resourceful, fully adapted to the art of self-preser-

4

vation. Every man was part blacksmith, gunsmith, carpenter, cobbler, miller, and tinkerer. A neighbor's skills often rounded out the services that were needed on the family farm. The small stores around the village were the center of commerce, where people traded by barter on occasion and held an account for long credit against their crops.

Cotton brought twelve cents a pound, high enough for a family to survive with dignity in spite of the less than a half-bale per acre yield throughout the Coosa Valley. There were three sawmills at various locations near the village, each employing a small crew of men. The few jobs with the sawmills and the railroad exhausted the range of employment available in the area. An adequate number of merchants and tradesmen offered the services needed for a basic agricultural economy.[15]

Two medical doctors and an assortment of ministers, a daguerreotype artist, and the faculty of teachers at the Cross Plains Institute were the only professional people in the village. Most of the county's legal and professional business was conducted in Jacksonville thirteen miles away, leaving little need for these services in the smaller towns.

Human drama was unknown to the people of Cross Plains. The rural environment was routine and uneventful. The family worked, hunted, went to church and parties, and expected to be buried in a small family cemetery and come to the Judgment Day to receive their reward together. Even when the Civil War raged about, no important battles were fought in Cross Plains. General John Croxton's raiders burned the railroad depot and iron works at Oxford and occupied Jacksonville long enough to release the prisoners in the county jail. Part of Sherman's army fought minor skirmishes in the Ladiga and Goshen communities near the village. But the

5

townspeople never directly felt the wrath of the Union army.[16]

Though little of humanity's bane and color surfaced in the hamlet of Cross Plains, 350 people lived there. Most of them wanted to forget a war that had disrupted their lives.

# I I

# The Morning After

THE THREE MEN who came to Cross Plains to recover the body of William Luke were apprehensive of the stillness in the hamlet. None of them felt fear of the community, but they expected a more restive and hostile atmosphere. On the morning of 12 July 1870, the town was as quiet as if a storm had passed violently through, leaving the people silenced by a supernatural fury. The streets were vacant except for an occasional white man. The heat and humidity of midsummer were unrelenting. The bright, torrid sun made the deserted, parched streets as uncomfortable as they were still.

Henry Brown, Charles Pelham, and William Savery were surprised by the quiet and calm of the village. Earlier that morning in Talladega, when the three men were notified of the hangings, and later on the train to Cross Plains, they had envisioned scenes of bedlam and human devastation. Aware of the Ku Klux Klan and its wanton disregard for northern men and blacks, they were prepared for the worst. The trio felt conscious of their notoriety as they made their way around the edge of the village. Since being deposited near Cross Plains by the driver of a hired buckboard, they had moved cautiously.

Early that morning, Henry Edwards Brown and his family were preparing for a new week at Talledega College fifty miles south of Cross Plains when a messenger from the railroad depot brought them the news of Luke's murder. The young school president hurriedly assembled his traveling companions and caught the next train north. Their concern that they might be in danger in Calhoun County was well founded. After the three men boarded the train, they passed through a smoking car where they overheard a man say: "Yes, we got Luke, Brown's satellite. We'd rather have had Brown—couldn't get him."[1]

It was near noon when they arrived on the outskirts of Cross Plains. They rode the train as near the town as they dared before hiring a buckboard to take them the rest of the way. By the time they arrived in town, the driver had told them what he knew about the hangings.

The men realized that the outward calm was deceptive when they tried to talk with some of the townspeople. They were told where the hangings took place but little else. Their questions were met with silence or, sometimes, the person queried simply hurried away.

Once the buckboard driver turned back toward Jacksonville, the men faced the problem of reaching the site of the hangings. Upon learning who they were and what they wanted, no one would lend or rent them a vehicle to claim William Luke's corpse. They walked on in the heat, sensing the scorn in the glaring silence of the townspeople who watched them from the secrecy of their shops and homes. The town was tense with rumors. People were unsure of what had happened the previous night, unsure of whom to trust.

Henry Edwards Brown knew he and his companions represented all that the South had come to loathe and despise in recent years. He knew southern whites called the northern people at the Talladega school "NT's— nigger teachers." The members of his staff were unable to rent rooms from any of the white families in town, and the food for the school was shipped into Talladega by friends or relatives from other parts of the country.[2]

The dark-bearded Brown had been in Calhoun County before. In November 1869 he had visited Patona, a small railroad town near Cross Plains. Invited by the railroad officials to discuss a relationship between the school at Talladega and the Selma, Rome, and Dalton Railroad, Brown had enjoyed a pleasant visit. The superintendent of the railroad had cleared out one of the warehouses at the headquarters and sent out announcements in Patona for a religious service that night at which Henry Brown preached.[3]

Brown was from Ohio, a graduate of Oberlin College and an ordained Congregational minister. He came South after the war in the rush of politicians, teachers, and preachers whom the southerners eventually called carpetbaggers. His decision to help educate the newly freed slaves following the Union army's victory was not an impetuous adventure. Brown had been a student at Oberlin at the time of Abraham Lincoln's assassination. When the funeral train passed through town the president of the college, evangelist Charles Grandison Finney, prayed an impassioned prayer on behalf of the Negro race. Overcome, young Henry went back to his room, fell on his knees, and dedicated himself to a life of service helping blacks overcome their disadvantaged past.[4]

During the war he had traveled through the Union lines with the Christian Commission, an organization

Henry Edwards Brown, founder and first president of Talladega College. (*Talladega College Historical Collections*)

that offered spiritual help and encouragement to the troops. After the surrender, when the American Missionary Association began to establish schools for freedmen throughout the South, Brown joined them in founding the school at Talladega. When Brown became president of the new school and moved his small family to Alabama, it was with the attitude of a missionary, not a conqueror.[5]

The tall man with Brown was accustomed to the noonday heat. He was a native southerner, a former resident of Calhoun County. Judge Charles Pelham was well known to the people of Cross Plains. Blond and graceful, Charles bore the family resemblance that made all of Dr. Atkinson Pelham's sons recognizable in the county. Charles's younger brother John, called "the gallant Pelham" by General Robert E. Lee, was the county's most revered Civil War hero.[6]

Charles Pelham also had served in the Confederate army. After the surrender he returned to his law practice in Talladega and brooded in the bitterness of defeat about the state of affairs in Alabama. One day, after weighing all of the possible risks, he announced a fateful decision to his family: he would join the Republican party. Not content to let the Yankees and the blacks control all aspects of local life, Pelham was determined to influence state politics. The Pelham family was indignant. Charles was violating an unwritten southern code of scorn by linking his political fortunes with the hated Republicans. His brothers were so infuriated that they turned their backs on Charles, vowing they would not even attend his funeral.

Changing his political alignment was a bold move for Pelham. When he signed the compulsory statement of allegiance to the Republican party, he knew he faced a barrage of scornful slurs. He knew too, that his family

11

would have to suffer personal abuse because of him. He was a traitor to the South—a scalawag.[7]

In spite of the loss of esteem and the continuing pain of public ridicule by his fellow southerners, Pelham benefited from the change of parties. Within a year he was appointed district judge for Talladega County. In time he was elected to the United States Congress.[8] Judge Pelham also became the confidant of Lewis E. Parsons, another Talladega resident, who may have been a factor in Charles's party switch. Parsons was the provisional governor of Alabama in 1865. The two men became political allies in the Alabama Republican party and were involved in many struggles to free the state from corruption.[9]

Charles Pelham's friendly attitude toward the new freedmen's school and his family's influence in Calhoun County prompted Henry Brown to appeal for his help early that morning. He thought Pelham would be useful in Cross Plains.

The third member of the trio symbolized the primary issue of the ongoing national crisis. He was William Savery, a black carpenter from the Talladega school.[10] As a slave Savery had labored to help build the Baptist Male Institute, an elite high school for white boys. When the war ended he was one of a group of freedmen who organized the first school for blacks in the area. Two years later he realized a personal dream when the impressive three-story building that he had helped erect became the administration center and classrooms for the new Talladega College.

William Savery's presence on the streets of Cross Plains, braving an atmosphere of racial tension, was the final gesture of loyalty to a new friend. When the Reverend Brown returned from vacation in Ohio the previous summer, an angular stranger in foreign, heavy clothing accompanied him. He was William Luke. The new arrival taught at the school until the president decided he was needed to help finish the construction of Foster Hall, the first dormitory to be built at the college. The cornerstone had been laid a few weeks before he arrived on the campus. While Luke was working on the building, the two men became friends. Luke's work on the dormitory daily brought together the two men from very different cultures who were to discover a common motive for their labor. Their friendship grew when Luke joined the Congregational church that Henry Brown organized after he founded the school. Luke quickly adjusted to the methods of worship and became an earnest and valued member of the integrated congregation.[11]

The versatile Canadian made an immediate and lasting impression on Savery. After Foster Hall was completed, Luke became a clerk in the school office, and through time the friendship between the men grew deeper. When Savery heard the news of Luke's death that morning, he asked to accompany Henry Brown to Cross Plains.

The persistence of Henry Brown and his companions finally achieved results. Beginning to anticipate failure in removing the body back to the railroad depot at Patona, they welcomed a change of luck. One of the townspeople offered them the use of a large four-wheeled cart built to be drawn by oxen. Although the cart was slow and exposed them to continued danger, the men were grateful to the owner, who also helped them construct a crude coffin for Luke.[12]

Thus meagerly equipped, the trio began a labored trek to the main street that would lead them to the place where the hangings had occurred. Soon the road curved to the left and fell into a shallow valley, then straightened

13

to rise again to the north and Cherokee County. When the party reached the curve, they were three-fourths of a mile from the crossroads in the village. Two hundred yards farther, beside the road, they came to the dreaded end of their journey.

From three medium-sized oaks, the naked ends of three ropes hung, stark and shocking, and men who had recently experienced the hell of war or the torment of slavery halted in awe of the death scene. They were silent for a time, as motionless as the quiet that dominated the grove of oak and pine.

The homes on the main road of the village were scattered, but here there were no houses, and the dense summer foliage hid the distant farms from view.

Moving toward the trees, the men noticed that the grass was beaten and most of the small bushes were freshly broken. The ground was worn with the trampling of boots and hooves and strewn about were the blackened remains of several wooden torches. The deathscape was completed by a rail fence that had been carelessly erected at the base of one of the oak trees. Only waist high, it enclosed the prone bodies of five men.

As Brown, Pelham, and Savery stood at the perimeter of the crude, barbaric pen, they noticed that some care had been taken with the bodies. Rather than being tossed impetuously over the fence, as other details around them might suggest, the bodies were arranged, democratically, in a row—a hat respectfully in place over the face of each dead man. Luke was in the middle.

They did not know any of the four black men in the pen. It was the white man lying in the gray, powdery dirt who drew their somber attention. He was William McAdam Luke, who for the past six months had worked for the railroad and lived in the village of Patona, a mile

14

west of Cross Plains. Before coming to Patona, he had been in Talladega since his arrival from Canada the previous summer.

A piece of paper was wedged under a splinter in one of the top rails. Henry Brown picked it up out of curiosity, thinking perhaps it was from the hangmen, and unfolded it. It was a letter from Luke. After showing it to the others, Brown retrieved the letter and placed it in the pocket of his coat.

In funereal slowness the yoke of oxen creaked back to Patona, to await the down train to Talladega. Brown worked quickly before their departure to collect Luke's personal belongings. First he went to the house where Luke had rented a room from a black family. There he found a large trunk that he recognized as the same one Luke had brought when the two men returned to Talladega the previous summer. Then Henry went to the offices of the railroad headquarters and showed the letter he found when he removed Luke's body. The railroad officials gave him a sum of money, more than $200, money Luke had saved since beginning work with the railroad.[13]

The Reverend Henry E. Brown preached at William Luke's funeral in Swayne Hall the next day in Talladega. The service was well attended by his friends at the school and members of the Congregational church. Judge Charles Pelham obtained a plot for Luke in the city of Talladega's public cemetery, Oak Hill, in the section reserved for blacks. Amid threats and abusive language from some of the local people, Henry committed the hanged man to the earth. Later Pelham had a stone erected over the grave.

The bodies of the other four hanged men remained in the grove at the edge of Cross Plains. Their families were not allowed to claim them from the pen. Two days after

William Luke's tombstone, Oak Hill Cemetery, Talladega, Alabama.

the hangings they were taken away by the sheriff and buried in paupers' graves by the county.

Later that summer, Henry Brown took William Luke's trunk, including the last letter Luke wrote his wife that fateful night in the grove, and delivered it to Fanny Ann Luke in Artemesia Township, Canada. A brief letter in mid-July had notified Mrs. Luke of the tragedy. Brown gave the aggrieved widow a personal account of Luke's success in Alabama and of the promising work he had started at Patona. It was agreed that the martyred schoolteacher—in spite of his short career there—had achieved his goal in the South.[14]

# III

# William Luke's
# Introduction to Alabama

✝ HENRY BROWN'S ARRIVAL in Alabama to assume the presidency of Talladega College could best be described as awkward. It was midnight, 20 October 1867, when the Reverend Brown and his wife Lucy came to the city. The lateness of the hour prevented them from finding their quarters at the school, and they spent the night in a hotel. The next day Henry took his pregnant wife and young daughter Bena to find the president's home at the school. They were given two low-ceilinged rooms on the second floor of a small dwelling that housed both students and faculty.

Immediately after his arrival, Henry Brown left for Montgomery. He had in his possession $8,000, the price of the school. The Freedmen's Bureau and the American Missionary Association had arranged for the purchase of the Baptist Male Institute, previously a select school for white boys. It was to be the only school for blacks in a nine-county area.[1]

Thirty-nine AMA missionaries were commissioned to work in Alabama that year. Three of them were sent to Talladega to help the Browns. Henry began the school by organizing a normal department and visiting the countryside to ask community leaders to "pick out the best specimen of a young man you have for a teacher, and bring to church with you next Sunday all the corn and bacon you can spare for his living, and I will take him to my school and make a teacher of him."[2]

Students were enlisted wherever they could be found. On one occasion Brown took a tent he received from New York and with four of his students went into the mountains to build a church and school for the people to help "them turn from the superstitions that had led them into such strange ways, to walk in the path of holiness."[3]

The school at Talladega opened with 140 students who, after finishing the third grade, would begin instructing the lower levels in the school. The enthusiasm for education had been kindled by the Cleveland (Ohio) Freedmen's Aid Commission. Two years before the Browns came to Talladega, a school for blacks had been opened, laying the foundation for the larger school.[4]

When the students returned to their homes in the summer, they were expected to teach in the communities. Training teachers became the most urgent work of the school. "Every intelligent 'grown up' student must at once be prepared to teach. We train these Normal students by carefully drilling them in the rudiments of two or three of the most needed branches," Brown wrote for the *Freedmen's Reporter*. He went on to say that "nine months of such training in the elements makes of an earnest person a more than average teacher for these schools."[5]

In the minds of the white southerners, the major flaw in the northern missionaries was their religious extremism. The same teachers and their societies that had formed the backbone of the abolition movement became the leaders of the educational movement. Societies like the American Missionary Association felt that their teachers must be fired with missionary zeal to withstand the pressure of living and working in a hostile environment.[6]

The North sent many qualified men and women to labor among blacks in the South. Although some may have been fanatical, many were not, and their efforts in black relief, education, religion, and economic self-improvement were based on a deep concern for the condition of the freedman. The motives of these teachers were misunderstood by southerners. Regrettably, however, they took some actions that alienated the races and clouded their genuine purpose for blacks. Overall these men and women felt they contributed to the total improvement of blacks by training leaders and raising their value as producers and citizens, generally making them a more capable people.

The poor whites, who made up about one-fourth of the white population, deeply resented the Negroes, the only group of people they could look down on as being inferior. Why should blacks get an education they could not afford for their children? Tuition for the Cross Plains Institute ranged from two to four dollars a month, less than the cost of sending a student to a similar school in Jacksonville. Because the economy kept many whites from obtaining an education, considerable conflict arose whenever a freedmen's school was established.[7]

At the Talladega school the students received more than an education. The material development of the school required as much of their time as the classroom. "I can get the students to do the work," Henry Brown wrote, "and so help them." He emphasized personal improvement through self-help. "I want them to get as much of books as they can," he wrote to Reverend E. M. Cravath, secretary of the American Missionary Association, "and get in addition an idea, a willingness, yea, a desire to do anything they can by way of self-support."[8] Brown believed that the education of blacks should stress practicality as well as piety. He helped to establish five Congregational churches in Alabama, but nothing in his work suggested radicalism. He seemed more concerned with correcting unfavorable conditions in the black community than with emphasizing religion or ideology.

Brown instituted an academic curriculum and a rigorous "set" of examinations. There were classes in Latin and Greek, geography, grammar, arithmetic, and analysis. One Talladega newspaper praised the college as one of the most successful institutions in the South.[9]

William Luke came to Alabama because of his chance meeting with Henry Brown. His move could not be called destiny, nor should it be thought of as fortunate, for certain it became his doom.

To alleviate the acute housing shortage at the fledgling school, the new president began a building program to erect a dormitory. Funds were raised from several out-of-state agencies, and an elaborate ceremony commemorated its beginning in early summer 1869.

After the cornerstone-laying festivities for Foster Hall, on a day the sun totally eclipsed, Henry Brown returned to the North. He spent several days resting near Lake Erie, a brief vacation from the rigors of his demanding work. At the conclusion of his vacation he left for Alabama by way of Cincinnati, where the offices of the American Missionary Association for the southern region were located. The dormitory project required equipment and supplies not available in Alabama. The school was making its own brick near Swayne Hall, and the Jewell family was sawing lumber for the framing

Foster Hall, the first dormitory at Talladega College. William Luke helped oversee its construction. (*Talladega College Historical Collections*)

material. Brown had with him an estimate of items needed to complete the building: quarry stone, doors, windows, and a range of hardware fixtures. The Reverend Cravath, AMA field superintendent for the South, would help him arrange for the purchase and shipment of the materials to Talladega.[10]

When Brown stopped by the association offices on Elm Street in downtown Cincinnati, an unexpected introduction provided him with a traveling companion back to the school. A lank Canadian named William Luke had appeared earlier at the AMA rooms inquiring about the work of the association. He had introduced himself as a teacher and requested information about a suitable field where he could start a village school for freedmen.[11]

Henry Brown's sudden appearance in the rooms gave the AMA officials a sterling example of the association's work among the freedmen. The energetic young minister personified the strength and character of its southern operation. The Reverend Brown launched into an enthusiastic report of Talladega College and what had been accomplished in a short period of time. He described for Luke the attractiveness of the school property, the progress of a large dormitory that was currently under construction, and the continuous flow of eager students who filled the rooms of the new school. It was, Brown related, the only school for blacks in a large area of northern Alabama.

Brown's unique educational experience provided an invaluable opening for the inquiring Canadian. The plight of blacks in the South was dire and urgent; the opportunities were unlimited. But Brown had also experienced the distressing problem of local resistance to those who helped the former slaves. Those who came to help "would be pushed out of a white society and have a very lowly work to do," Brown would counsel others in later years. There would be "no fame . . . only plenty of hard obscure work." They prayed, and Luke said he would go to Alabama with Brown.[12]

The prospect of a new success intrigued Luke. In addition to starting a freedmen's school, the teacher was also interested in making a home for his family, who had remained in Canada. Talladega and the gentle Alabama climate were appealing. Once he was settled, his family could join him.

Since it would take time to make arrangements for the building materials, Brown told the new recruit that they would not return to Alabama for several days. Luke had been traveling for over two weeks and was short of funds. Because of the unexpected delay, he took temporary work at a nearby lumber yard to provide for himself until Brown's business was completed.

During the trip into the heart of Dixie, Luke showed his employer a letter of recommendation from his pastor in Artemesia Township, Ontario. William Luke, the letter said, had been a dedicated member of the Wesleyan Methodist church of Canada since boyhood; the last few years he had been the superintendent of its Sunday School. The pastor was generous in his personal praise of Luke, outlining his qualifications as a teacher, Luke's profession in recent years. The letter, in Christian kindness, did not refer to any former position in the church, and Luke made no mention of it to Brown.[13]

The journey to Alabama was long and strenuous but pleasant because of the company the men provided for each other. They shared similar interests, and their conversation was soon filled with the spiritual concerns that ordinary men found boring and uncomfortable. By the time they arrived in Talladega, Brown and Luke were friends.

They arrived amid the flurry of activity around the building of the large dormitory. Foster Hall was beginning to assume an imposing size when Brown delivered the materials. The dormitory was badly needed to replace several private homes that were housing the students.

Initially, Luke was not involved in the project but was given teaching duties in Swayne Hall across the street. Later he became instrumental in its completion when he was made the timekeeper and overseer for the ninety workmen who were hired by the school. It was during this period that Luke became friends with William Savery, one of the school's incorporators and original trustees. After Foster Hall was completed, Luke kept books in the school office.

Swayne Hall, the administration building at Talladega College where William Luke taught. It was the site of his funeral. (*Talladega College Historical Collections*)

"We soon found him a faithful and earnest man," Henry Brown remembered later, "doing with his might whatever his hands found to do. He readily adjusted himself to our modes of prayer meeting and Sabbath School, and became a working member of our church."[14]

# I V

# William Luke
# as Minister

✝ WILLIAM McADAM LUKE was twenty-four when
  he began his ministerial career with the Wesleyan
Methodist church of Canada. He had come to Grey
County, Ontario, from Tyrone, Ireland, early in his life
with his parents, John and Jane McAdam Luke. The
great potato famine had forced the migration of poor
but industrious Irish citizens, trying to escape their broken existence. North America became home for thou-
sands of Irish families.[1] Arriving first in Owen Sound on
the Georgia Bay, the Luke family moved twenty miles
southward into Artemesia Township and began a new
life in a new world. It was a hard, rugged existence, but
the family prospered in the primitive north woods.

William's religious inclination was evident early in his
life. The log church near Flesherton, which was little
more than a frontier mission when the Lukes moved into
the township, seldom had an activity or service that
young Luke did not attend. After he had exhausted the
resources of the one-teacher school, William's interest in
books prompted his parents to send him to Owen Sound
to attend public school. His tuition was paid with fur

trapped in the great north woods and produce from the Luke farm.

Luke's return to the farm after finishing his intermediate education was spent helping his father. William's pastor, sensitive to the young man's desire to continue his education, lent him books from his small library. The pastor also entrusted the leadership of the young people in the church to Luke. It was in this capacity that William Luke met Fanny Irwin on an outing for the youth of the Wesleyan Methodist churches in the township. Fanny was younger than Luke and a member of the Markdale assembly.

Like the Lukes, the Irwin family had migrated from Ireland. Alexander and Francis Irwin were from Sligo and had moved to Canada in 1849 to settle in Artemesia Township. They were more prosperous than their neighbors and built a home that was uncommonly large for the township. Alexander Irwin became a magistrate and was known around Grey County as Squire Irwin. Methodist services were held in their home for some time after its construction, and the Irwin family eventually donated land to build a church and cemetery at the edge of Markdale.[2]

William Luke's courtship of Fanny was at all times happy and promising. The couple saw each other at regular intervals over the next two years, whenever a church activity brought them together or when Willam traveled the five miles to Markdale.

It seemed almost predictable that William Luke would apply to the presiding elder of the Wesleyan Methodist church for a position in the ministry. His years of service to the church and his devout application of his religious experience to life seemed to indicate such a career. Luke was received on trial with the church in 1855. In the beginning he served as a part-time preacher in Owen Sound under the watchful eye of the presiding elder. When he was properly satisfied with the young minister's diligence, the elder assigned him to a small pastorate in the township of Proton, a few miles from his home. The next year he pastored in nearby Elora. The following year, 1858, was to be an important one in William Luke's life.[3]

The church officials were pleased by Luke's hard work at his ministerial assignments. They decided he was ready for a larger ministry and sent him to Wallace, to be the minister of a moderate-sized church in central Ontario. The new pastorate was encouraging, but the crowning act in his ministerial career came in June, when Luke was received into full connection by the church. He was ordained at the Thirty-Fifth Annual Conference of the Wesleyan Methodist Church of Canada, which was meeting at the Great Saint James Street Wesleyan Church in Montreal.

Flushed with success in the rise of his career, Luke rushed back to Artemesia, where he married Fanny on 17 June. The wedding was an important event because of the prominence of the Irwin family in the township and Luke's professional reputation. Guests from several of the townships in the area attended the wedding, including William Kingston Hesherton, member of the Canadian Parliament. The Reverend Thomas Culbert performed the ceremony.[4]

Luke returned with his new wife to the Zion Wesleyan Methodist Church in Wallace near the village of Trecastle. For the next three years they lived handsomely in the one-and-a-half-story house, a fine parsonage compared to the log houses occupied by the farmers around them. A year after the newlyweds came to the modest church, a son, William Alexander, was born. Two years later they would have a daughter, Fanny.[5]

Wallace was then a wilderness area with only a few settlers, many of them recent immigrants from Germany. The mission work was difficult, but the new minister attacked it with vigor, as the following report from Luke to the *Christian Guardian* in December 1858 attests:

Although this mission may be nearly, if not altogether unknown to most of your readers, it will nevertheless be gratifying to those of them who love and sustain our mission work, to hear that God is reviving his work among us. Shortly after our last Quarterly meeting in Burk's Neighborhood, we commenced a protracted meeting in the usual way, but God has more than usually blessed us. Between forty and fifty have professed saving faith in Jesus, the most of whom have already united with us. Although the meeting lasted four weeks, there was no dimishing of interest no falling off, but rather a steadily increasing power and interest until the very evening, which was the last evening of the meeting, no fewer than nine souls were savingly converted to God. To Him be all the praise. We are all rejoicing here now. The wilderness and the solitary places are rejoicing—the church is rejoicing—sinners are rejoicing and singing, "O for His love, let rocks and hills their lasting silence break." All are rejoicing except a few members of another church, who, in spite of all their hostility, have been sadly disappointed by seeing the "spread of righteousness" through the agency of Wesleyan Methodist.[6]

Luke's three-year tenure at Wallace was followed by an appointment to the prosperous farming community of Point Abino on Lake Erie. The Reverend Luke and his family were the first to live in a newly purchased frame house, one of the few parsonages in the Niagara District.[7]

Luke's previous success with mission work at Wallace had attracted the attention of church officials. In the Wallace pastorate, Luke had successfully controlled a rash of hostilities against the Methodist church by members of the German community. This experience made him the natural choice for a new mission. In the summer of 1862 Luke assumed responsibility for a German mission near Eganville, a desolate area in the cold, rugged Ottawa Valley. Even though it was a wilderness area, with no parsonage available to house the family, no chapel in which to worship, and few members, Luke's family faithfully accompanied him to his latest assignment.[8]

At first Luke responded to this new challenge with his usual enthusiasm, as the following excerpt from a letter to the *Christian Guardian* sent by another minister at a nearby mission reveals:

> Bro. Luke is indefatigable in his work. I will give you a short quotation from a letter I received from him this evening. . . . "My visit to Arnprior last Sunday, and crossing the Ottawa on Saturday were of no little interest I assure you. We were several times at the mercy of the storm while on the river, and it was only after an intense struggle of three quarters of an hour and the assistance we got from land, that we suceeded. I never worked harder in my life . . . but God was greater than the storm . . ." Bro. Luke is the right man in the right place.[9]

The approving observation of Luke's fellow minister was soon tested. Eganville—isolated and strenuous—would be the setting of Luke's professional failure, blighting a career that he had prepared for since his youth and tainting his reputation in the church and township.

At the next meeting of the Pontiac District of the Wesleyan Methodist church in Pembroke, a German family petitioned the conference with a charge of adultery against Luke. The German Lutheran community at Eganville, bitterly opposed to the establishment of the new Methodist church, had directed a relentless barrage of hostilities at the new mission and its pastor. Luke's error in fidelity provided the community a chance to deliver a fatal blow to the church.

So firm was their evidence that the district officials resolved that "the charges preferred against W.M.C. Luke are fully sustained." He was suspended from the ministry until the ensuing district meeting, which also recommended that "W.M.C. Luke be deposed from the Christian ministry and expelled from the church."[10]

Luke did not defend himself against the charges.

The Fortieth Annual Conference of the Wesleyan Methodist Church of Canada, which met in Quebec City on 11 June 1863, upheld the decision. The following year the charge was further investigated by the church to ascertain its validity. Ultimately, the decision was made to sustain the recommendation to expel Luke from the church at the next annual conference in Toronto.[11]

William Luke left Canada in late July 1869. His brother-in-law, the Reverend William Irwin, also a Wesleyan Methodist minister, last saw him on the road near Artemesia Township. In their conversation Luke related his plans for a new career. Irwin recalled, "He told me he was going to the United States and if opportunity afforded he thought of going to the South to teach. He was a man of good education and address and was able to fill a good position as a teacher." Luke said that as soon as he was settled in a permanent position, he would send for Fanny and the children.[12]

More than five years had passed since the final decision had been made about the immorality charge at Eganville. In the meantime Luke returned to Grey County, Ontario, and made a home for his family that had grown to six children. He found a job teaching school, and he and Fanny resumed their membership in the local Wesleyan Methodist church, where he became the Sunday School superintendent.

Luke adjusted to the stigma of his excommunication. He offered no defense nor made any public explanation for his conduct. He went stoically forward with his life, conscious of his family's dependence on him. The shame of Luke's moral flaw did not dissolve his relationship with Fanny. She remained loyal to him and, like their religion, continued to be a source of comfort and assurance.

In spite of Luke's successful recovery from disgrace, he remained unsatisfied. He had based his ministerial career on more than hope for professional success. William Luke harbored a real desire to serve humanity, to wrestle with man's deepest spiritual problems. That desire did not wane after he was forced to leave the ministry, and his work with the church and Sunday School did little to fulfill his need.

The trauma of the American Civil War had been felt even in the farthest reaches of Canada. For years secret pipelines for fleeing blacks emptied across the borders into the provinces, and the Canadian press followed the brotherly travail with a personal effectiveness. When masses of blacks were freed across the South, illiterate and without direction, Canadians knew of them and their conditions.

It was a restless William Luke who studied the plight of blacks. Unreconciled to his teaching profession, he and Fanny weighed the opportunity to teach in a more meaningful way—to be a missionary among the destitute freedmen. The move would be difficult. Luke would have to find an organization that specialized in black education, secure a position, and then prove himself in the South. In time, when he was settled on his new job, the family could join him.[13]

William Luke was five miles from his home in Artemesia Township when he met his brother-in-law. As they talked in the road, Luke expressed what he hoped to accomplish in the South. William Irwin never saw him again.[14]

# V

# Ku Klux Klan
# Terrorism

✝ IN THE SPRING of 1868, while the Reconstruction
governments were forming, the Ku Klux Klan
spread throughout the South. The civil terror that
gripped Talladega, Cross Plains, and the rest of the
South was predictable. Those who initiated the Reconstruction process should have known that retaliation and
resort to violence would occur whenever southern honor
was insulted, its power base threatened, or the social
balance jeopardized.

In Calhoun County night riders from a den in Jacksonville prowled the countryside, menacing blacks, Union
men, and local scalawags. For a time the Klansmen operated as a well-disciplined, military-precision guerrilla
force, drawing from their battlefield experience. But the
continued success of their violence, unthwarted by the
military or local law enforcement officials, made them
bold. Many Klansmen harassed their victims unmasked
and in full view of their fellow citizens.

The constant nuisance of the Klan prompted Thomas
Fister, Jacksonville attorney and the county's Republican
representative to the legislature, to request troops from
General Samuel Crawford, commandant of federal

forces in Huntsville. Colonel Conrad, with a cavalry unit and a detachment of infantry, came to Jacksonville in September 1869 and patrolled the county's northern end until March 1870.[1]

The presence of federal troops failed to stop the local Klansmen from conducting their clandestine activities. A group of the county's Republican officeholders wrote to Governor William H. Smith complaining that the county was experiencing the worst state of lawlessness since the close of the war. The letter cited recent incidents in which the Klan had raided Negro quarters in Alexandria, shooting one man in the leg and whipping several others. The sheriff arrested the white men, but they produced witnesses to prove their innocence. On the same night as the Alexandria raid, another party of Klansmen searched for a notable scalawag, John DeArman, the county treasurer. Fortunately, DeArman had left by train on a fishing trip.

> There is scarcely a day or night but that some acts of violence are committed on some person or persons within our county and who are beaten and ran off and sometimes murdered. And threats of violence and intimidation are of constant weariness. There has been a large number of families driven off from their homes within the last twelve months, and threats and intimidation have caused others to remain and labor where they do not want to stay.
>
> It does not make any difference what act of violence on a member of the Republican party whether he be black or white, nothing can be done with him. It is utterly impossible for the civil law to be enforced in this county.

The letter was signed by W. P. Crook, clerk of the circuit court; county commissioners Elias Stephens, J. K. Napper, W. W. Crook, and Issac Frank, with John A. DeArman, county treasurer. All of the officials were white Republicans.[2]

This appeal was one of many from over the state for Smith's help in quieting the chaotic political situation. His opponents placed the blame for all of the Ku Klux outrages at the feet of the young governor, and the much maligned Unionists and Republicans accused him of abandoning them to the fury of the Klan.

Governor Smith did not ignore the problem of violence in Alabama. He made attempts to find a solution, but none proved to be effective. Initially he depended primarily on harassed citizens' prompt reporting of crimes, and if necessary, joining a posse to aid the sheriff in suppressing violence. But the hit-and-run tactics of the Klan and the sympathy of the white population discouraged such public support.[3]

The governor also urged local civil authorities to become more aggressive by making more arrests and by forming a posse whenever the need arose and to report those who refused to join. When local support was not forthcoming, the authorities were to call for federal troops for assistance. Smith believed that as long as a community tolerated violence without punishing the offenders, the situation would continue to worsen.

After William Smith entered office he saw two laws to suppress Klan activities passed by the Radical legislature. The first measure provided heavy penalties for the wearing of masks or disguises, especially for committing violence in such attire. Anyone killing or wounding a disguised person who was engaged in violence was exempt from punishment, and local officials who failed to prosecute such offenders were liable to a fine or removal from office.

36

The other law made it possible for victims of Ku Klux atrocities or their next of kin to recover damages up to $5,000 from the county whenever Klan offenders were not prosecuted or convicted. It mattered little what laws were passed, however, for the civil courts did not function in Klan cases.

Lacking power to form a state militia or to declare martial law, Governor Smith passed the responsibility back to the local communities. Underestimating the dimensions of the conspiracy, Smith failed to recognize the inability of local authorities to deal with systematic terrorism. One angry scalawag complained to the governor that the carpetbaggers had "already landed everything that is Republican in Hell."[4]

The federal troops, in constant demand from their station in Huntsville, were seldom effective in calming Klan unrest. Even though twenty thousand troops were stationed across the South, they had limited authority to aid local officials and intervened only when asked. The military found it fruitless to arrest the Klansmen: the authorities refused to prosecute them, and the courts and juries refused to convict them. The presence of the troops embittered the whites, and conditions often worsened after they left.

Colonel Conrad's troops in Jacksonville did little to quell the violence, and their presence provided another form of deception for the Klansmen. The *Jacksonville Republican* noted, "Some of that awful Ku Klux Klan and some Negroes had a fisty cuff and a general rough and tumble time of it a few nights ago. From the scraps of old blue cloth lying around with the loose wool, we judge they must have been disguised in Federal uniforms."[5]

Federal troops were able to provide reasonable protection for northern interests in the county. In May 1870,

Captain E. G. Barney, superintendent of the Selma, Rome, and Dalton Railroad in Patona, foresaw problems with the Klan if the infantry unit that was left in Jacksonville was removed to Huntsville. Barney petitioned General A. H. Terry for protection to prevent acts of lawlessness against the railroad personnel. Barney explained the railroad's indefensible position: "As we are now situated we would be comparatively powerless should any of these threats be carried out with execution by a band of disguised ruffians who are willing to take almost any steps to rid this section of men who are true to the government and its laws and have no interest in politics." He ended his plea by asking for troops to protect the railroad headquarters at Patona.[6]

No troops were sent despite Captain Barney's repeated requests to General Terry and Governor Smith. In late June, railroad employees, mostly northern men, were the target of a den of Klansmen who operated from Ladiga, a small community about four miles above Cross Plains. In the dead of night, the disguised riders shouted threats to burn the railroad's buildings and shrilled the rebel charge as they raced through the yards.

Another officer of the railroad pleaded with the governor for help: "We are at the mercy of a lawless set of persons who are bold to threaten and have an organization sufficient to do as they will." The harried official observed, "We are respected by the better class, but it is the ignorant short sighted and those blind to the interests of the country from whom we expect persecutions and danger."[7]

Fifty miles south of Patona the fury of the Klan was just as intense. The freedmen's school in Talladega stood isolated and defenseless as the night riders plundered and ravaged the countryside. With no federal troops stationed in the city, the school was a lonely Yankee outpost between Montgomery and Huntsville. The Klan viewed the black school with anger. When the young blacks returned to their communities to start rudimentary schools, many of them were beaten, shot, or run out of the country and their buildings burned. Five Klansmen took Irving Jenkins prisoner while he was teaching at a school ten miles from Talladega. Grasping an opportunity "he sprang from them into the bushes and escaped," stated a report from the school. "They fired several shots and wounded him. They burnt his schoolhouse."[8]

Another act of brutality was directed against a family that supported the school. The J. E. Jewell family from Ohio had moved to a farm near Talladega and set up a sawmill to cut timber for AMA work. Mrs. Jewell's elderly father, Deacon Coe, came South with his daughter and gave the association a large farm three miles east of Talladega. The family worked the mill for more than a year until one night it was burned, apparently by the Klan. The planing mill and the sawmill were a total loss; the boiler and mill engine were salvageable.[9]

May Jewell wrote to the Reverend Cravath about the tragedy that destroyed their dreams.

> We hoped soon to finish paying for the groceries you supplied us with, but Sabbath morning our mill was set on fire and was burned to the ground. We have payed something, but have been out of water for some time and have been hard pressed, but we hoped to work our way through. This has taken the property we had worked so hard to pay for. I would be glad to pay up (as far as it will go) with what I am to have from Father as soon as he can get it for me. The Lord has taken this work out of our hands that we thought he wanted us to go into, and now we long to go into the Christ work and give our life to it if you have any place for us.

39

We came South hoping for this but the way did not seem open, but we have felt that we loved to be more constantly at work with the people. Please let us know *soon* if you have any use for us where we can get a living.

Oh when will the workers for Jesus be free from the reign of these Ku Klux. Pray that the Lord will show us where we can do the most for Jesus.[10]

Shortly afterward the Klan decided to burn the school. For a week Klansmen tried to incite trouble between whites and blacks in Talladega without success. When the Klan made its move on the school, blacks rallied and sent word that if the buildings were destroyed they would burn the town. "Altogether the prospects are very encouraging," Justus Brown wrote about the school, "except the danger from the Ku Klux. From all that I can gather I think there must be a dreadful state of things in this state."[11]

# VI

# A New Start for
# William Luke

✝ THE RAMBLING DORMITORY at Talladega College was completed in the fall of 1869. Workers labored to finish the building in time for the opening of the new school term. William Luke continued as overseer until the construction was completed and the rooms filled with students. Then he went back to Swayne Hall as a bookkeeper in the school office.[1]

In the meantime, Captain E. G. Barney was directing the completion of the Selma, Rome, and Dalton Railroad. Large crews of whites and freedmen labored at a rapid pace in Alabama and Georgia to finish the remaining miles of track, which the superintendent had promised the board of directors would be completed by the end of the year.[2]

The future of the line occupied Captain Barney. An employee would be needed to manage and maintain the new road. In addition, Barney would need "to obtain a permanent and reliable class of labor," workers trained in the operational skills of a railway system. He realized that many of the employees would be freedmen, in line with the railroad's policy to hire freedmen and northerners preferentially.

In late 1869, Captain Barney projected his labor needs. A school would need to be started "to improve the minds and morals of the negroes." The school would begin modestly and grow as the new railroad town developed.[3]

Patona was the headquarters of the railroad company and the general offices of the A. D. Breed Company, builder of the line. The railroad had owned the property for about a year when Captain Barney went to Talladega in late fall 1869. The older portion of the railroad, which had been completed before the Civil War, ran through Talladega, affording the superintendent influence and reason to visit the city. Captain Barney wanted to visit the freedmen's school on the western side of town.

The superintendent arrived in the middle of the fall term and introduced himself to the school president, Reverend H. E. Brown. Barney was familiar with the American Missionary Association and its work in the South. Like Henry Brown, he was from Ohio, the home state of many AMA missionaries. The meeting went well. Captain Barney offered "to cooperate with the A.M.A. in educational and religious matters" and explained his desire to start a school for blacks at Patona. The school would prepare students for Talladega College, and employment with the railroad would be available to them upon graduation. Both the college and the railroad would benefit.[4]

In the course of Barney's visit, he was introduced to William Luke and given a glowing report of the Canadian's earnestness and good work. The presentation immediately took a positive turn when the superintendent, "wishing a bookkeeper in his office at Patona, desired Mr. Luke for that position." Luke seemed a particularly good candidate because "it was deemed politic to occupy as many points as possible along the railroad where a

Sabbath School might be formed." A Sunday School could "eventually develop into a church, and Mr. Luke would have opportunity to organize such a school." The superintendent and the school president decided to talk further about the arrangement. Henry Brown would visit Captain Barney and inspect the facilities at Patona.[5] Brown visited the railroad headquarters on the first day of November 1869. When he arrived from Talladega by train, Brown found a frenzy of building in the small railroad town. Bricklayers were raising the walls around temporary warehouses and shop buildings. Tree stumps on the perimeter of the village witnessed the remains of a dense forest.

The superintendent showed Brown around the head-quarters property and described the company's plans for further development. The machine shops in Selma would be moved when the buildings were complete, and in an area nearby housing would be built for company personnel. The plans also called for a church and a school.

The site had been chosen because of the availability of iron and the nearby coal fields. Investors were impressed by the vast outcroppings of brown hematite ore near Cross Plains and had bought the large tract of land for mining purposes. Barney told Brown there was a vein of ore so rich that it could be dug from the side of the mountain. This deposit was less than a mile from the depot.[6]

Afterward the two men outlined the program they had discussed at Talladega. Their plans centered on the Canadian Barney met at the school, whom the captain envisioned as a combination employee-missionary. The position would involve primarily clerking in the company office, but there would be other duties. Luke would organize a Sunday School for black children and hold preaching services and prayer meetings. The position would be extremely demanding, but Barney expressed confidence in Luke's ability to handle it. The superintendent also agreed to pay the salary of a female AMA missionary when the school was large enough to justify another teacher.

Captain Barney offered to help the Talladega school train telegraphers, who would eventually be given positions with the Selma, Rome, and Dalton Railroad or other lines that were opening in Alabama. This program would add another dimension to the school. Henry Brown said he would begin the class as soon as the necessary equipment could be obtained.[7]

Brown was elated as he made the fifty-mile train ride southward through Jacksonville, Blue Mountain, Oxford, and Munford. Through this exciting turn of good fortune, the state's largest railroad company was guaranteeing jobs for some of his students, but more important, the school was gaining a reputation in the state.

Brown enthusiastically gave William Luke the good news that the railroad wanted to hire him as a bookkeeper and teacher. Henry Brown told Luke that the job would require "a man of brains and push equal to Henry Ward Beecher," the popular preacher, who favored a moderate Reconstruction program.[8]

Although he had taken other duties since his arrival in Talladega, Luke had not lost his primary hope to minister to the freedmen. The position was the fulfillment of Luke's original plan to start a village school for freedmen. If Captain Barney's school was successful, Luke's family could move South. Luke's background in religion and his experience as a teacher made him doubly qualified to be the superintendent's extraordinary railroad clerk. He told Henry he would accept the position.

Late that November night, Henry Brown wrote to the field agent of the AMA, telling him the school had been able to make these special arrangements because "Supt. Barney prefers live Christian men in his employ." Soon several normal students from Patona would come to the school, Brown wrote. "I wish I had more railroad and other business men here to recommend to the openings." Brown related how Barney had cleaned out his depot and himself circulated notice of a meeting and attended with others.[9] Henry Brown preached at the Patona meeting.

The problems associated with Reconstruction had little effect on the expansion of the railroad system in Alabama. The construction of the Selma, Rome, and Dalton Railroad, the largest in the state, continued in spite of the violence throughout the state.

The depot in Jacksonville, an impressive two-story brick structure with living quarters, opened for freight and passengers even before the road was completed to Georgia. Abel D. Breed of Cincinnati, Ohio, had been awarded the contract for finishing the one hundred miles of road from Blue Mountain to Dalton, Georgia. At the urging of the board of directors in New York City, work began in both states. More than two thousand workers, most of them freedmen, labored to complete the road.[10]

The original franchise for the line called for its termination in Gadsden. But the northern capitalists who assumed control of the unfinished road after the war thought Gadsden was a point of no importance because it lacked connection with any other road. The industrialists changed the course of the road at Jacksonville to connect with other lines and form a link in the direct chain of railroads between New Orleans and Washington.[11]

Several Calhoun county residents held positions of importance in the railroad company: Thomas A. Walker of Jacksonville was a director and later became president; William H. Forney was a major stockholder; and George M. Chapman was elected by the board of directors as secretary and treasurer at an annual salary of $2,500.[12]

The corporate offices of the railroad were in New York, and the majority of stock was owned by investors in New York, Cincinnati, and Europe. The Astor family controlled a large block of stock and installed Franklin H. Delano, a relative by marriage, as the company president.

The business of the railroad was handled primarily by Captain E. G. Barney, a patient, tireless man in his mid-fifties. The title of captain resulted from his once having been a member of his local militia. As superintendent of the road and general agent of the A. D. Breed Company, he divided his time between the one-hundred-mile construction site, Breed's offices in Cincinnati, and the Wall Street offices of Franklin H. Delano.[13] Captain Barney did not escape the stigma of the carpetbagger label given to northern men. His involvement in Alabama industry failed to spare him the customary defamation, in spite of the enormous power he wielded in the state. Because his company was building other roads in Alabama, he represented a formidable financial empire.[14]

Barney believed there was a need for Christian grassroots involvement in the southern recovery process. He used his position with the railroad to hire freedmen preferentially and to give northern missionaries free railroad passes to travel the line at will.[15] His initial visit to Talladega was an instance of Barney's foresight. The hiring of William Luke assured Patona of a school and religious services that would help provide moral and educational influences for blacks who worked for the railroad. Anticipating the new work among the freedmen, the superintendent alerted the other railroad officials of Luke's role with the company.[16]

When William Luke left Talladega, he realized that he was leaving a sanctuary that offered reasonable security and safety. He was perplexed by the scorn of some southern whites toward him. Many of the citizens around Talladega were tolerant of the new school and encouraged its success. Others, however, harassed outsiders and approved of the terrorists' preying on the Yankees. Luke learned to be cautious when he left the school family.[17]

Luke settled in Patona during the first week in December and wrote his family about his new position with the railroad. The clerk's job required him to learn the skill of telegraphy. He described the job to Fanny and told her that Captain Barney had provided him space for a school in the commissary building. The black families had been notified that Sunday School and church services would be held each week.[18]

Luke surmised that if his new venture went well, Fanny and the children would be able to join him soon. His letter included a short prayer of gratitude: "Father I praise thee for thy protection and care over the wife of my heart and youth and over the children thou hast given me." In closing he referred to himself as "Your own old good for nix, William."[19]

On Christmas Day at the railroad yards in Patona, Luke was alone among the festive southerners. Upon his arrival from Talladega, he had rented a room in the Patona Hotel, a small rooming house near the railroad yards. He had been there only a few days when a group of angry citizens told the proprietor that he was a "nigger teacher" for the railroad. Luke was asked to leave. The act of ostracism failed to discourage the Canadian. He found lodging with a black family who lived near the railroad yard. On that cold Christmas day he wrote to his "Dearly loved and loving wife" and told her of his loneliness.[20]

When word spread that he taught black children for the railroad, Luke was shunned when he went to the post office in Cross Plains to collect his mail, and the townspeople began to refer to him spitefully as "Old Luke." But his letters home and the occasional notes he sent to Henry Brown revealed no hint that he was troubled by the hostility he met.

Fanny Luke, concerned for the family of a recently deceased friend in Grey County, wrote her husband of the widow's grief. In late January Luke responded, suggesting that his wife remain a faithful friend, "for her and for the sake of him that is gone. Many years ago when I first commensed to preach, I found much strength and comfort from Isaiah 41:10; Do. 42:16 and yet another verse I have partly forgotten, you can find it." Remembering what he could of Isaiah 43:2, Luke penned words of encouragement from the Old Testament: "When thou passeth through the waters, I will not overflow thee: when thou walkest through the fire, thou shalt not be burned; neither shall the flame kindle upon thee." The closing lines of the letter gave evidence of the deep emotional bond in their marriage: "My ever dear wife, my own sweet loving Fanny, again goodbye till next we meet. Faithfully and with a heart full of love, I remain your own, ever and ever, William."[21]

The lone Canadian found no friends in Patona. Most of his co-workers were northern men who had been brought South by the railroad company. Reflecting the prejudice of some northerners toward blacks they scorned him. They hid his telegraph key at night to prevent him from practicing and cursed him repeatedly for minor problems at the headquarters building. He met no better reception at the depot in Jacksonville. Luke helped hire railroad gangs for the line and traveled from station to station occasionally, often stopping in the county seat. Threats and curses made his visits to the depot uncomfortable and embarrassing.

Whenever Captain Barney was away from Patona on business, some of the northern men secluded themselves in a room in the commissary where Luke taught the Sunday School and howled and banged on the walls to disrupt the classes and frighten the children. Once they barred the door of the commissary from the outside, and Luke had to crawl through a high window to let the children out.[22]

Luke's estrangement from local affairs became more pronounced as time passed. Early in 1870, Henry Brown rode the train up to Patona to visit with his friend. When Brown arrived at the depot and asked for Luke, he was told that no one by that name worked for the railroad.[23]

James Cowan, a young Talladega minister, encountered a similar problem when he tried to find the teacher on an overnight visit. He was met with silence from other railroad employees before locating Luke. Their visit was marred by cursing and lewd singing, "an exhibition like a young pandemonium, swearing, filthy jests and songs, as bad as I ever heard in a groggery," Luke said. The two men eventually left the depot building to walk on the loading platform and "without interruption, enjoyed an evening's communion together by the light of the stars."[24]

# VII

# Community Antagonism
# to William Luke

✝ THE NEWS SPREAD among the three Klan dens in
northern Calhoun County that Luke was teaching
racial equality at Patona. It was rumored that he told
blacks that they should ask for the same wages as white
laborers. The scarcity of farm labor in the county
prompted the chairman of the county agricultural committee to recommend "cultivating only the best lands" to
counter the labor shortage.[1]

Klan sympathizers within the railroad company
monitored Luke's classes and reported what he taught
the black children. When Luke told the children that a
black woman was as good as a white woman in the eyes of
God, rumors were spread about the county that he had
fathered several children by Negro women during his
stay in Alabama. These rumors alarmed the white population, and an aura of hate began to form around his
name. The quick temper of the people made it difficult
for the harried teacher to travel very far by himself in
that part of the county.

The Klan singled out William Luke for surveillance.
Klan partisans inside the railroad company—even northern men—supplied the terrorists with information about

the Canadian teacher. At the signal of two quick pistol shots, Klan members would gather and debate how to get rid of Luke.

On 20 March 1870, Luke rode the train to Jacksonville to attend a new church for freedmen at the edge of town for which he had organized a Sunday School. He stopped by the studio of Edward Goode, a ferrotype artist on the town square, and had a photograph made of himself. Displeased because there were dark specks around the eyes, he requested another. The same defect recurred, and Goode explained that the specks were caused by the shaded area at the corners of his deep-set eyes. To obtain a good likeness and capture the light of his blue eyes, the photographer suggested that another picture be made with Luke's head turned slightly to one side. Luke declined and bought the first picture, re-marking that it was the only picture he ever had made of himself.[2]

Luke planned to stay overnight at the Old Hotel on the west side of the town square. He planned to hire more workers for the railroad the next day. When Luke entered the hotel to take a room for the night, he was confronted by a group of angry men. A hulking railroad switchman, Bob Lodge, also an employee of the Selma, Rome, and Dalton Railroad, pushed Luke. Two weeks earlier Lodge had threatened Luke in Jacksonville, shouting epithets at him in the crowded waiting room of the depot. Lodge and twelve to fifteen of the local Klans-men followed Luke into the hotel, intent on preventing him from getting a room. Voices rose in anger as the men assailed Luke for teaching blacks how to turn their freedom to their advantage.

Luke appealed to James Hammond, the hotelkeeper, for protection. Hammond knew Luke and had rented rooms to him on several occasions when he came to

Jacksonville on railroad business. But Hammond remained silent, preferring to avoid involvement in the fray. The heat of their anger growing, the men shouted that Luke was meddling into their affairs; he had no business telling blacks about wages and schools and the Bible. Someone said Luke had been seen hugging a Negro woman. These words inspired a new round of curses and accusations.

In the four months Luke had been in Calhoun County, much of that time spent within the black community, he had heard the rumors that were circulating about his activities. New lies and half-truths appeared regularly. He failed to understand how and why the people thought up untruths about him, and he felt despair at the total misunderstanding between himself and the local community.

When the harassment began, Luke determined not to dignify the rumors with a reply or resist his taunters. He had come to the South to help the freedmen, and he considered himself fortunate to have the position with the railroad. On this Sunday morning, however, for the first time he was alarmed by the invective that was displayed toward him. He was threatened with being run out of the country if he did not stop teaching Negroes.[3]

The ultimatum from the Klan did not stop the schoolteacher. Before he left the hotel lobby to catch the late train back to Patona, Luke told Lodge and his companions that he had no intention of quitting his job. The next week he received word through Tom Anderson, a friendly employee at Patona, that the Klansmen were spreading the word that they were going to "Ku Klux" him.

Luke did not mention the face-to-face confrontation with the Klansmen in his next letter to Fanny. His venture into the South had been undertaken with great hope, and he shared the excitement of his new position but not the fear with Fanny in each letter he wrote to her. To tell her of the trouble he was having would cause her unnecessary concern. Instead, Luke sent the photograph he had made that Sunday in Jacksonville—the only photograph she ever had of her husband.[4]

Luke's letters to Fanny, full of endearments and advice, were a poor substitute for the reunion of the family, whom Luke was unable to send for as quickly as he had anticipated. Although his position with the railroad was secure and seemed more promising as time passed, he could not subject his family to threats and insults. The money he sent with the letters provided adequately but not luxuriously for them. Alexander Irwin, Fanny's father, promised to see to the family's welfare until they could join him.

Initially, Luke reasoned that he would be accepted by the southern whites when his role in the black community was fully understood. He was convinced that once they realized his true intentions, they would receive him in their society and he would be able to attend to his duties in peace. At that point, his family could join him. But Luke's optimism soon dimmed.

Only days after the Klan issued its heated demands, Governor Smith and General Crawford came to Jacksonville to investigate the almost daily complaints their offices were receiving about Klan activity in the city. When the officials visited the railroad depot, Luke was there hiring workers for the company. Anxious for details about the local terrorists, Smith and Crawford listened to Luke's tale of his encounter with the Klan. On hearing about the threats he had received at the hotel, they advised Luke to complain to the local authorities and report the incident to the superintendent of the railroad. Reluctantly, Luke petitioned the spring term of the county grand jury that was in session, telling about the existence of the Ku Klux organization in the county and his experience with it. The panel was asked to fulfill its lawful duty and rid the county of the terrorists.[5]

When the grand jury called him to testify, Luke had already returned to Patona. A deputy was sent to bring him back to Jacksonville. In the courthouse in the middle of the town square, the grand jury examined him about the Klan, but Luke refused to give any information. He even declined to name the men who had threatened him at the Old Hotel that Sunday in March.[6]

Luke's hesitance to identify the Klansmen was a sign of the personal trauma he was experiencing. As long as there had been only rumors, he was content to go about his normally peaceful duties. But the incident in the hotel was different. He had seen hate in the eyes of the vicious Klansmen, and their thundering demand that he quit teaching blacks still rang in his mind.

Luke reported the incident at the hotel to Captain Barney in a four-page letter dated 29 March 1870. The letter began with an apology: "I have ever since a boy detested telling tales on others, or blowing my own horn, preferring to suffer a present temporary wrong that the truth may vindicate itself." Luke explained that he was writing at the insistence of Governor Smith and General Crawford and that he must defer to the opinions and advice of these experienced men. In relating the hotel scene to the superintendent, Luke referred to the men as ruffians and told of their threat to run him out of the country if he did not stop teaching black children. "I of course refused to comply with any such terms and dared them to interfere with me and my peaceful and uninter-meddling duties." He named Bob Lodge as the leader of the Klansmen. Luke revealed for the first time some of the problems he was having at Patona: "In order to carry out your wish I applied myself to the study and practice of telegraphy. To do this I would go downstairs of an evening to practice on an instrument on a small table in the middle of the room. Then would commence a commotion of vile cursing and threats until I would have to leave."[7]

He also told Captain Barney about the time when the door to his school in the commissary building had been locked from the outside. Luke told how, after beating on the door and calling for help, he had to slip out a high window and unbolt the door. The telegraph operator, a Mr. Sanders, was sitting by the door cleaning his shoes. "I asked him who locked the door when he flung at me a torrent of oaths as I have seldom heard, and ordered me not to speak to him in any way." Luke wrote that he "could relate more but I forebear. I have been treated with a considerable lack of friendliness which is so common among men having the same common interest." He concluded, "I do not find fault—I have probably fared better than I deserved."[8]

The railroad was occupied with moving company headquarters to northern Alabama. The move from Selma to Patona was a complex process. Personnel, records, and equipment had to be transferred without interfering with the operation of the line. At the time Luke was hired by Captain Barney, the headquarters was a skeleton operation, having recently occupied the newly built railroad village. The fifty men who helped in the initial move to Patona lived in barracks, eating at a common table and working extended shifts because of a lack of personnel to staff the new headquarters. Bricklayers were toiling from sunup to sundown, bricking around the wooden framed shop buildings and constructing warehouses for equipment that was arriving weekly.[9]

The most imposing part of the company's property that remained in Selma was the machine shops, an extensive operation that maintained the train engines and rail cars. They were saved for last, to be shipped to Patona in one exhausting effort when the hulking, cavernous buildings were finished and the final phase of the transfer was complete. The movement of these machine shops was of considerable interest at the annual stockholders' meeting held at Patona, 9–11 June 1870. The business meetings had been conducted in Selma in the past, but the impending final shift of equipment to northern Alabama prompted the board of directors to schedule the convention at the site of the new headquarters so they could inspect the operation at Patona.[10]

Three trains had converged on the small Alabama hamlet by Thursday, 9 June. From Selma came two cars of stockholders with the Honorable John W. Lapsley and General Levi Lawler, directors of the company; Colonel Daniel S. Printup and a contingent of stockholders from Rome and Dalton arrived at midmorning. The last train to arrive illustrated the reason why the company wanted to change the direction of the pre–Civil War route from Gadsden to a more northeasterly course. A private rail car left New York two days earlier, linking with various lines until the train reached Dalton, Georgia, and connected with its own road. On the train were some of New York's elite businessmen: Franklin H. Delano, president of the company and namesake uncle of Franklin Delano Roosevelt; A. G. Mabry and U. A. Murdock, Wall Street investors, and William Paton, the most active director in the business of the railroad and the man for whom Patona was named.[11]

Activity around the railroad town was spirited and busy the week before the convention. Accommodations were made for the visitors; the president and the mem-

Franklin Hughes Delano, president of the Selma, Rome, and Dalton Railroad and representative of the Astor family fortune. (*Franklin Delano Roosevelt Library*)

bers of the board of directors were quartered in the homes of company officials at Patona. The buildings were trimmed and groomed, and the site of the meetings, the depot, was hung in colorful bunting. Freedmen dug a long, shallow pit in the train yards, and Captain Barney supervised a barbecue that cooked overnight. The largest grocery house in Rome, Georgia, Pitner and Smith, catered the feast.

The stockholders' meeting was festive. "Joy was unconfined," the *Jacksonville Republican* noted. The road was completed well within the time required by the contract, and Delano reported that a bill had been presented to Congress, confirming and ratifying the land grants provided by the original railroad charters. The Senate had already passed the bill, he said, and the measure was presently in committee in the House of Representatives, fully assured of final passage. The railroad president also told the convention that the board had transferred the right of franchise and the road beds from Jacksonville to Gadsden. A new railroad company organized by William H. Forney, James Crook, John Everett, Peyton Rowan, and Thomas A. Walker would link the two towns.[12]

On Friday morning a delegation of public officials and private citizens from Jacksonville arrived by train to lobby for the location of the machine shops in their city. James F. Grant, publisher of the *Republican,* was impressed by the collection of industrialists. In the next issue of his paper he wrote that "every countenance indicated a shrewd businessman as the bearer—some even approaching crafty."[13]

Between business sessions Barney escorted the stockholders on walking tours of the new town site for company employees. Several hundred people would be moving to Patona within the next year. The superintendent explained that Patona and the one thousand acres owned by the railroad were in the center of rich iron deposits and coal fields, necessary components for the industrialization of the South. The railroad company was making a major capital investment that would total into the millions of dollars to create the new town and help rebuild a region that they believed would bloom with prosperity in the future.[14] In his office Captain Barney served wine and brandy to his guests and showed them on a set of maps on the wall the position of the machine shops and plans for a new foundry. The development of Patona would be lengthy and exhaustive.[15]

Cross Plains was little more than a spectator to the color and energy of the convention. With no government structure to function officially, the people remained aside in silent deference as the industrialists conducted business about which the natives of Cross Plains knew little, unaware that a city was being created that would rival their community as well as all of the other cities in northern Alabama.

When the convention concluded its agenda on Saturday morning, the delegation from New York remained in Patona until Sunday. The delayed departure was a boon for Luke. On Sunday morning Captain Barney invited the northern capitalists and their wives to visit the commissary and the makeshift school that was taught by William Luke. The superintendent wanted them to see firsthand this special facet of the railroad's involvement in southern Reconstruction.

Luke had prepared his children. They did recitations and sang, demonstrating an enthusiasm and a capacity to learn that impressed the New Yorkers. Before the private car left on the long journey northward, arrangements were made to build a schoolhouse for Luke and the children before the village was completed.

Within a week Captain Barney received an indignant letter from Franklin Delano. A member of his party had learned through his wife that the white teacher and his school were the subjects of ridicule and harassment by some of the northern men at Patona who resented his work among blacks. The agitators were fired and sent home.[16]

In mid-June difficulties in the life of the dispossessed minister seemed to moderate in favor of his Christian adventure.

# VIII

# Violence Erupts
# in Cross Plains

✝ SOON AFTER THE superintendent removed the
Klan sympathizers from Patona, the most serious
threat to Luke's life occurred. Late one night, at the
home where the teacher kept a room, a handful of
pebbles rattled the window; seconds later a pistol shot
exploded into the room. The throwing of the pebbles
was a ploy to arouse Luke from sleep, causing him to sit
up in bed. The only lives endangered were those of the
elderly black couple huddled in their bedroom on the
opposite side of the house. Luke was in Jacksonville with
members of the new freedmen's church.[1]

Luke wrote the governor about the attempt on his life.
In March he had been asked to notify the state officials if
he had any more problems with the Klan. In a few days
Sheriff J. W. Williams went to Cross Plains to investigate
the complaint. "I called upon various citizens, law abid-
ing men, who gave me their version of the difficulty in
that section, and who gave me every appearance of their
willingness to aid me in enforcing the laws," Williams
wrote to Governor Smith.

The sheriff did not see William Luke that day, but the
local citizens assured him that the Klan was not a prob-

lem in the town. The first week in July, Sheriff Williams told the authorities by letter that everything was under control and that only a few minor incidents had occurred, none of which were serious.[2]

About the same time Henry Brown received a note from Luke, almost jesting about the attempt on his life. "You may yet have to write my obituary," Luke wrote, before ending the letter, "Yours in the Lions den."[3]

The failed mission incensed the Klan because its members had not known Luke would be out of town that night. A meeting was called of the dens that roamed the northeast part of the county. From virtually every community within a fifteen-mile radius of Cross Plains, Klansmen assembled at a Baptist church in the Goshen community just across the Cherokee County line.[4] The meeting was subdued. There were no lofty, flaming crosses or ghoulish regalia. It was simply a meeting of "the Organization," a collection of men who opposed causes that were contrary to their way of life.[5]

The Klansmen selected a twelve-member execution squad from the assembly to plan another attempt on Luke's life. This time nothing would be left to chance. Some of the men volunteered quickly and eagerly. Others stepped forward out of a sense of duty. The death squad included two brothers who were former Confederate soldiers, the den leader from Jacksonville, a seventeen-year-old who was known for his quick, violent temper, and a Baptist preacher. The remainder were farmers who lived in Ladiga, Spring Garden, and Nancey's Creek.

During the meeting a rider on his way to Gadsden became curious about the churchyard full of wagons and horses. The men at the door refused to admit him, and the stranger feigned illness to gain entry to the meeting. He had not been seated long before someone recognized him as a Union sympathizer from Tecumseh, a community near the Georgia line. Three Klansmen removed the curious intruder from the church and escorted him to his home.[6] The meeting ended without any announced assassination plan. The details would be worked out by the squad, who received an unwritten contract, time, and the blessings of their fellow Klansmen.

Green Little was lounging on the shaded side of the Cross Plains depot when Patrick Craig, aged seventeen and drunk, rode up on a mule and thrust the reins into the black man's hands. He then joined a group of his friends loitering on the loading platform. The depot was a meeting place for the local young men. Attracted by the new railroad, they spent their leisure time sprawling on the platform, making idle conversation, and occasionally passing a jug. That evening the young men were drinking, and the people walking to the evening service of the Methodist church could hear their raucous laughter.[7] Little resented being a lackey for anyone, especially a quarrelsome bully like Craig. While a slave, Little had been a discipline problem for his master, William Washington Little, a farmer and a member of the secession legislature from Cherokee County. After the emancipation, Little roamed the countryside, working only when necessary and living wherever he could at Tobetown, a small concentration of black families on the northern side of Cross Plains. Green was teased by the blacks about the well-known fact that his former master was the head of the local Ku Klux Klan.[8] The southbound train sounded in the distance, and the mule jerked at the reins. Green Little called for Craig to come get his animal as the six o'clock train

Southern Railway Depot, Piedmont, Alabama, site of the Selma, Rome, and Dalton Depot where the fight occurred that started the Cross Plains tragedy.

approached the busy village crossing and blew its whistle shrilly. The mule, normally kept on the placid Craig farm, bolted and ran down the road toward White Plains.

The enraged Craig jumped from the platform with an eruption of curses and bowled over the black man. Little, dazed and furious, scrambled to his feet with a sizeable rock in his hand. This time the white boy sprawled in the dust. Retreating to a stack of firewood beside the platform, Craig seized a length of wood and began clubbing Little.

In the meantime, the train grated to a halt by the depot, and a group of freedmen passengers gathered by the windows, attracted by the noise and excitement. They saw a circle of white men pushing, kicking, and hitting a lone black man. More shouts and oaths were added to the din as the freedmen rushed from the train to join the fray. Before they could reach the other side of the platform, the station agent came out of the depot office with a shotgun, scattered the whites, and forced the blacks to get back on the train.[9]

A beaten and bleeding Green Little edged away from the white men, cursing and vowing revenge. Craig, sobered, started down the road to White Plains in search of his mule.

The fight at the depot should have ended there and would have if the prevailing mood had been more rational. But it was a time of change and turmoil. Many southerners had not learned to be civil or humane to the Negro, and the Negro did not fully understand the fragile limits of his new freedom. The ruling passion, the result of a disordered society, was a manic struggle for power and survival.

Green Little returned to Tobetown incensed by the abuse he had suffered at the depot. He retrieved an old pistol from the room where he was staying and in the dusk of summer's evening started for Patona. Little did not have any trouble rounding up several loyal friends to help vindicate himself. In a short time a group of ten pistol-toting black men collected around a flickering lantern beside the narrow road to Cross Plains.

The sound of their heated talk alerted the residents, who, on learning their intentions, sent for the white schoolteacher. William Luke attempted to dissuade them from going to Cross Plains and settling the score. He cautioned them that an attack by armed blacks on the white village would bring quick reprisals from the Klan, not only for them but for all blacks in the area.[10]

Little moved his gang down the road and into the darkness before Luke could talk any of them out of going to Cross Plains. The party of blacks walked quickly, excitement mingled with their anger. In a few minutes they were at the crossroads in the village, where they found a group of white boys loitering by the public well. Little decided that they were not the ones who had beaten him earlier in the afternoon, and the boys scurried for home. The gang of blacks continued their search, boasting loudly and making threats as they moved down the main street.

C. J. Sharp, owner of a store at the crossroads, heard the commotion from his home behind the store and walked around to the front in time to see the gang pass. Puzzled by the sight of armed blacks boldly patrolling the streets, Sharp went back to his house and lay across a bed by the window to watch the crossroads.[11]

About the time the storeowner discovered the band of blacks, a daguerreotype artist, E. L. Hesterby, returned to town from asking the doctor to visit his sick wife. It was eight o'clock as he neared the crossroads and saw the party of armed blacks milling around the main intersection in a state of excitement. Stealing closer through the shadows of the store buildings, he heard one of them say, "Boys, let's go back." Another replied with an oath that he had come to attend to matters and would do it before he left; that he did not intend to be run off.

The photographer took a seat on the porch of Dailey's Store to wait for the doctor to come into town, when Oliver Dukes, an employee of the Cross Plains House, came running through the crossroads. When he saw Hesterby he asked him if he had seen any black men. The photographer told him that a group of them had just gone down the White Plains road. Dukes said they were plotting to get the whites who had beaten Green

Little that afternoon. Dukes ran to the hotel to tell his employer, and Hesterby went to the Methodist church to alert the congregation of the plan to attack the white boys.[12]

The people in the church were alarmed by the news but decided to remain in the safety of the building. During the fluster caused by the photographer's announcement, four young men in their late teens slipped out of the back door and into the alley behind the church. Milton and Shields Keith had guns at home. With them was a still slightly intoxicated Pat Craig, the principal target of Little and his gang, and another boy who went along simply because he was asked. At the Keith home they collected two shotguns and a pair of revolvers and began circling the village in the shadows of the buildings. Now there were two armed bands roving the streets of Cross Plains— each looking for the other.[13]

Meanwhile, at the church, part of the congregation decided to risk walking home as a group to help ensure their safety. About twenty of them, mostly women and children, started down the street with men in front and back of the main group. Some three hundred yards south of the church, Craig and his party, who had made a broad sweep of the village emerged from the rear of a house near the crossroads. When the four young whites appeared from the shadows of the house, two of the blacks who were scouting ahead saw them and alerted the rest of their band with a loud, keen whistle. The signal brought Little and his companions from behind the blacksmith shop to see Craig and the other boys on the opposite side of the street, the Methodists between them.

"Here they are!" Green Little yelled, firing his pistol. The people from the church froze for an instant, as the blacks began shooting over or through the crowd at Craig on the other side of the street.[14]

Confusion reigned in Cross Plains for the next forty-eight hours. The women and children, who were heading for the safety of their homes and had been warned of the armed blacks, thought they were being attacked. The wadding from a pistol shot by one of the blacks tore through the sleeve of a Miss Farmer's dress, and she fainted. The men pulled her to the front of Johnson's store and crowded the others against the wall of the building, where they would be out of the crossfire.

The white youths held their fire momentarily while the church people scattered out of the way. Then Milton Keith yelled, "Charge!" and triggered a load from the double-barreled shotgun as the white boys set out in pursuit of the attackers.

The blacks ran behind the stores into the darkness, firing their pistols as they fled. The charge was halted for a moment when Little turned and fired several rapid shots, causing Craig and his friends to retreat to the rear of the store buildings. Little emptied his gun and yelled that his group was going back to get more men.[15]

Firing blindly until their ammunition gave out, Craig and his friends followed the blacks into the darkness. The black men raced through an open field on the Stevenson farm and hid among the outbuildings close to the rear of the house. Awakened by the sound of shooting nearby, Stevenson was standing by his bedroom window when he saw the moonlit forms of several men running across his field. By the time the blacks secreted themselves among the low storage buildings, Stevenson was watching them from the back of his house with a shotgun in his hands.[16]

When Craig and his friends shuffled back into the crossroads, describing how they had routed the attackers, the streets were beginning to fill with people curious about the gunshots. The women and children caught in the middle of the fight were helped to their homes, after it was determined that Miss Farmer had fainted and not been wounded.

Amid the confusion and questions, Stevenson walked into the intersection with a shotgun cradled in his arms and told the enlarging crowd that from the back of his house he had overheard some of the blacks say they wanted to return and finish the fight; they had called the members of their gang who preferred to flee cowards. They argued about what they should do next, Stevenson said, until one of them suggested they return to Patona "and get seventy-five well armed men and return and wipe out and burn the damned town."[17]

Panic was added to the confusion with this news that another attack could be expected. Several lanterns were placed in the center of the street, and the men gathered around it to decide how to protect the town.

One of the men suggested that an older man be selected to lead them, someone who would keep the young men from doing anything reckless or rash. S. D. Johnson, an elderly merchant who was highly respected in the village, was asked to be the leader, but he declined because of his age. The group next asked Andrew Bailey, principal of the Cross Plains Institute and a former major in the Confederate army. Bailey agreed on the condition that he have sole authority.[18]

Major Bailey's initial strategy was to prepare the town for another attack. Pickets were posted on the perimeter of the village to provide a warning; the remainder of the men were deployed in the center of town, ready to move toward the point of attack. They waited anxiously. After an hour, Bailey walked around the edge of town and talked with the advance guards. They had not seen or heard anything. The major then sent men to scout Patona and Tobetown, but they returned without having seen or heard anything suspicious. All was quiet where they had scouted.

After waiting another hour without any action from the blacks, Bailey sent a party of men to Tobetown to question the black families about the attack. This move gave the defenders momentum and direction. A black woman who worked as a housekeeper for a family in Cross Plains named ten men who had been in Tobetown earlier in the night, whom she said had tried to talk some of the younger men into joining them to make trouble in Cross Plains. Later the woman told her employer that she had given this information out of fear for his children, especially the baby girl that she had nursed since birth.[19]

When the men returned with the names of the attackers, Bailey scribbled a quick note explaining the town's dilemma and sent a boy on the next train to deliver it to the sheriff in Jacksonville. The nearest public official was Justice of the Peace Slade Nabors, a forty-four-year-old farmer at Nancey's Creek, five miles south of the village. Bailey asked him to come and serve as the magistrate for the sheriff.

Calculating that there would not be enough armed men to defend the town if a large force of blacks did return, Bailey dispatched couriers to Ball Play, Natville, and communities in Cherokee County to the north; Nancey's Creek and White Plains to the south; and Spring Garden and Pleasant Gap near the Georgia line.[20]

The activity in Cross Plains was not halted by the lateness of the hour. Torches and lanterns illuminated the central section of town, while men walked the streets in small groups, nervously fingering their hunting weapons, blaming the Yankees and the Republicans for fomenting black lawlessness.

Major Bailey, now certain of the identity of the attackers, decided to go after them. Afraid that they might try to escape by train, Bailey and ten volunteers boarded the southbound train when it stopped at the depot at two o'clock. As the train rolled slowly to Patona, Bailey dropped men along the tracks and told them not to allow anyone on board.[21]

The blacks did not try to get on the train as it moved toward Patona. As the engine picked up speed for Jacksonville, a railroad employee ran up to Major Bailey and told him that a wounded black was hiding in a cabin. Bailey crossed the tracks with the volunteers and found a black man peppered with squirrel shot. After harsh questioning, the man admitted that he had been with Green Little in Cross Plains. Bailey placed him under arrest and sent two men with him back to Cross Plains. As the prisoner was being carried off, one of the scouts shouted that a party of blacks was advancing on them.[22]

Afraid that another confrontation would erupt into more gunfighting, one in which the odds would clearly be against him and his men, Bailey walked up the tracks alone to talk with the blacks. As he approached them, he heard the sound of several pistols being cocked. Bailey identified himself and told them not to go any further, saying he was interested only in the men who had attacked the church people. The blacks stopped and eventually walked back to the edge of the tall pines and watched the white men from the shadows of the forest.

When Bailey rejoined his men, two black men ran across the open railroad yard toward the men who were holding the lone prisoner. The major ordered them to halt. As they did, each drew a pistol from his pocket, but the pistols snapped on empty chambers. Realizing they were out of ammunition, the two blacks ran toward the pines.[23]

71

Bailey and his men opened fire on the blacks. Shields Keith, armed with a shotgun, spun one of them around; the other made it to the safety of the trees. The wounded man identified himself as Jacob Moore; he was bleeding profusely from his buttocks and the back of his legs. Bailey's men helped Moore to his feet and prepared to take both of the prisoners back to Cross Plains, when they saw the blacks move out of the edge of the forest and onto the railroad tracks.

Giving orders to the men not to fire, the major stopped the advance of the gang of blacks by positioning the two wounded prisoners in front of them, while he acted as a rear guard, his pistol pointed toward the black men spread across the tracks as the white men passed through the armed blacks.[24]

It was dawn when Bailey returned to the village with the prisoners and found the streets teeming with armed white men who had come to Cross Plains at the alarm sounded by the couriers about the attack on the church people. They were eager to help defend the town against another attack.

The appearance of the wounded prisoners reinforced the belief that the town had been assaulted by a gang of blacks. Jacob Moore's trousers were sodden with blood, and the other prisoner limped into the crossroads; both bowed their heads in guilt. Armed men surrounded them.

A fight that should have ended early in the evening had grown into a night of terror and the widespread belief that innocent people had been attacked.

Slade Nabors waited by the old well for Major Bailey. With him was J. M. Steel, the bailiff of the beat; Nabors asked him to help with the legalities. The men who crowded around the public well to examine the two prisoners were angry, and for a while a suggestion passed among them to hang these two and go after the others.

Bailey showed Nabors the list of names that the woman in Tobetown had given the night before. It included Caesar Frederick, the wounded black who was taken from the cabin in Patona. When questioned by the justice of the peace, Frederick and Moore told Nabors that the men on the list were with them in the attack on the whites. At the insistence of the Keith boys' father, the civil authorities issued warrants for the prisoners. Nabors also signed warrants for the remaining men on the list, including several who were thought to be involved in the plot. Milton Keith told them he saw a white man in the raiding party, but Nabors refused to issue a warrant on the word of the boy.[25]

Because school was out of session, Bailey told Nabors and Steele that the prisoners could be held at the school building, which would also be a good place to conduct an investigation when all of the culprits were in custody. Bailey left for Patona a second time with a handful of warrants and a posse of fifty men.

The large force converged on the Negro quarters in Patona, spreading like an invading army among the crude cabins, questioning, cursing, and accusing. The large, angry posse was little more than an uncontrollable mob.

Two more of the attackers, Toney Cliff and Berry Harris, were taken from hiding in their cabins, but the remaining blacks on the list could not be found. The posse began systematically to collect every black in the small village. Bailey said they would be used as witnesses in the investigation.[26]

The posse assembled all of the blacks and began moving them up the road toward Cross Plains. They were just starting when Milton Keith, who earlier had tried to implicate William Luke, ran up to Bailey and pointed to a house behind the others, set at the edge of the trees. Luke was standing on the porch watching the spectacle.

"There's the man!" Keith said, pointing to Luke. "I think he's the one I saw there last night."

Major Bailey halted the posse and the throng of blacks and accompanied Keith to the house. Luke listened to Bailey's explanation of the attack and Keith's accusation that he had been with the gang of blacks. He admitted no guilt; he protested no innocence.

"I'll go with you and we'll investigate it," Luke said. He picked up a plain black hat from a chair on the porch and joined the posse.[27]

# IX

# The Trial and
# Klan Justice

✝ THE PEOPLE who waited at the Cross Plains Institute heard Major Bailey and the posse make their
way up the main street from the crossroads before they
could be seen down the tree-lined street. The sound was
the shuffling of many feet on the hard dirt street, of
iron-shod horses, and of saddles weighted with riders,
creaking in motion. The sight of the mass of people
nearing the school would remain forever in the memo-
ries of those spectators.

The posse filled the street, a small army of irregular,
plainly clothed men. On each flank were horsemen
herding what appeared to be every black in Patona. A
broad row of men, perhaps fifteen to twenty, walked
behind the prisoners as the rear guard. Behind them
followed another group of townspeople.[1]

The black witnesses were moved to one side of the
schoolyard, beneath the trees where the children played
when school was in session, and told to sit. The conspira-
tors in the attack were carried to the porch to join the
two wounded men.

William Luke had been the center of attention since
the posse left Patona. As the mass of people plodded

slowly toward town, the sight of the lone white man among the blacks, circled by armed men, sent a wave of vindictive excitement through the townspeople who watched them pass. The name "Luke" was spoken in low tones as he walked with the blacks toward the schoolhouse.

The prisoners and witnesses had moved slowly, surrounded by their captors, looking down or avoiding the contemptuous stares of the townspeople watching them trudge down the road. Luke had walked upright, his eyes recessed and shaded by the black hat. Luke was taken to the porch, where he leaned against the wall and studied the four men talking in the yard below him.

Major Bailey gave a summary of his foray into Patona to Nabors and Sheriff Williams. He was unable to find the chief culprit, Green Little, but scouts had been sent into the countryside to search for him. Another group of men had been dispatched to Tobetown to round up more witnesses.

Within an hour a small group of black men was added to the large number already seated under the trees, and the sheriff helped the justice of the peace make plans to investigate the attack.[2]

After all of the witnesses arrived in the schoolyard, Slade Nabors set the time for an investigation. Tired men rushed home to eat and rest before the meeting at the schoolhouse. The visitors who came to help defend the town were either invited into the homes of the townspeople or dined at and lounged about the Cross Plains House.[3]

The sheriff and his deputy took Luke into the dining room of the hotel, where a throng of people gathered around the table as the men took their midday meal. Sheriff Williams continued to pry information from Luke as they ate. During the meal Luke admitted his indirect guilt in the attack—he had sold a gross of pistols to the black men at Patona.

"I admit I have done the white people wrong," Luke said. The pistols had been sold "on speculation" several weeks earlier.[4]

Long before the proceedings began, the schoolyard filled with curious people who gaped at the frightened blacks and told everyone how the matter should have been handled. The street in front of the school was an impassable maze of farm wagons and buggies; horses were tied wherever their owners could secure the reins.[5]

The inquiry was held in the large classroom that also served as the auditorium for school activities. The windows were raised to abate the heat, but there was no breeze. When time came to begin the meeting, the packed room was hot and musty, the stillness dominated by a heavy scent that was distinctly male.

Slade Nabors presided over the hearing from the desk at the front of the room. Leonidas Ferguson sat at a small table beside the desk and kept a written record of the proceedings. Sheriff Williams and the bailiff held Luke and the black prisoners in custody between them on a long bench at the front of the room.

The people of Cross Plains were stirred by the capture of the attackers. The return of the posse with the mass of blacks and the much-talked-about white man caused great excitement, and rumors swept through the streets.

All but a few of the people who crowded into the large schoolroom thought they were attending a trial and would be able to observe justice applied to the violent blacks. They expected swift, decisive judgments that would ultimately end in the execution of the attackers.

A sequence of witnesses was called: Craig, the members of the Methodist church who were caught in the attack, and several members of the posse. When the witnesses finished their testimony, a substantial case for the prosecution had been established.[6]

Toward the end of the day, as the hot summer sun was losing its intensity in the western sky, the magistrate called William Luke to testify. Many of those who crowded into the schoolroom had only heard of the white man who taught black children for the railroad. His appearance at the school was their first glimpse of the hated Canadian.

The throng of people focused their anger and indignation on the lone white man. He was the primary representative of the current problems in the South. The rumor that Luke had incited the attack on the church people infuriated the townspeople and the men who had ridden in from surrounding communities to help protect the village. They wanted to know why he had provoked violence.

Luke's answers did nothing to fuel the rage of the people. He denied any part of Green Little's shooting spree in Cross Plains.[7] The teacher told all he knew about Sunday night's attack. Earlier in the day he had readily agreed to accompany the posse to Cross Plains to clear himself of any involvement in the gunplay. He had even revealed the previously unknown fact that he had sold pistols to the blacks in Patona. When he was brought to the witness stand, Luke told them what he knew of the events leading up to the attack. He explained to the court that he had been summoned to try to reason with the gang of blacks, but they had refused to listen and he was unable to stop them. Luke's testimony was supported by the prisoners, who told the crowd that he had asked them not to go to Cross Plains with Green Little.[8]

Luke's innocence should have been resolved by the word of the attackers. But the anger of the people demanded his guilt, and they refused to believe that his hands were clean. The investigation turned into an inquisition as the townspeople attempted to extract some fault—known or unknown—from the teacher. What was the nature of the meeting with the black men that he had called at four o'clock Sunday afternoon before the shooting? If he had prior knowledge of a planned attack on the town, why had he not warned someone?[9]

The issue at that point became larger than the attack, or Luke's guilt, or his failure to warn the town. The townspeople had within their grasp an object of their personal hate, a man favored by the power structure that scorned them.

The questions came in a rush, confronting Luke with rumors and gossip that burned in the mind of the community—all related to Patona and his role with the school for black children. Did he advise black farm workers and household help to seek the same wages as white workers? Was he aware that many of the landowners were unable to hire enough help to run their farms because of what he told the black laborers? Luke explained that he encouraged blacks to seek equal wages to improve themselves economically.[10]

Did he teach in his school that a black woman was equal to a white woman in the sight of God? Luke said that he did. This was the question that most interested the crowd. The only sin worse than integration of the races in the southern mind was racial sex. It was rumored about the county that Luke had fathered several children by black women since he came to Alabama. Luke denied the charge, pointing out that he had been in the state little more than six months.[11]

The attack also touched one of the more primitive fears of the southern people. Since the latter days of slavery, the threat of black insurrection had weighed heavily on the minds of the white people. The open manifestation of that fear was the unspoken rule that blacks must be kept in their place. When the gang of black men fired on the townspeople and followed the violence with a threat to return with seventy-five armed men and wipe out the whole village, fear triggered predictable hostilities and reprisals to suppress the surge of black lawlessness.

Where had the blacks gotten their guns? Green Little and his friends had been amply supplied with pistols, and all of the black men Major Bailey had confronted at Patona had firearms. The authorities were unable to learn from the prisoners the source of weapons, although Luke admitted before the open court that he had sold a gross of pistols to the blacks on speculation. He said the pistols were sold for the blacks' protection.[12]

The frightened prisoners were intimidated by the crowd of hostile whites and the verdict of guilt that was already assigned to them. The inability of the blacks to cope with the interrogation brought the white Canadian to their defense. Luke counseled them and helped his fellow prisoners defend themselves against their accusers.

In an attempt to support the prisoners, Luke relied on a well-known law enacted by the Radical legislature, which allowed all persons the right to shoot and kill anyone in disguise. During the examination, Luke asked the prisoners if they believed the Methodists—especially the women and children—were Klansmen in disguise. The black men said they thought the Klan was after them and they had simply tried to protect themselves.[13]

There was not enough time to complete the investigation on Monday evening. Before sunset came and the light faded in the schoolroom, Slade Nabors adjourned the proceedings until nine o'clock the next morning.

The magistrate told the crowd that more information could develop during the night.

Many of the men at the investigation were not satisfied with Nabors's methodic, thorough pace. Some of the disgruntled men slipped from the room in sullen disapproval and collected in small groups around the school, arguing among themselves about what should be done with Luke and the blacks.

Slade Nabors was not satisfied either. He adjourned the examination until the next morning to attempt to find further proof of the blacks' guilt and to weigh any new evidence that the sheriff might uncover. But Nabors's caution and sense of fairness were not appreciated. When the justice of the peace and the bailiff left the school grounds, they heard remarks about Luke and the blacks and how to dispose of them.[14]

The sheriff took custody of the prisoners for the night. When Jacob Moore began to moan and roll his eyes erratically, Williams asked one of the town's doctors to check him. After studying the encrusted wounds, the doctor said that Moore should not be moved because he probably would not live until morning. The doctor bandaged Moore's wounds and gave him medication. Sheriff Williams asked two of the blacks from Patona to stay with him in the school through the night and get him whatever he needed. The doctor said Caesar Frederick's wounds were not severe.[15]

Sheriff Williams was also faced with the problem of where to quarter the prisoners until the inquiry reconvened in the morning. Cross Plains did not have a jail. He asked W. S. McElwain of the Selma, Rome, and Dalton Railroad, who lingered in the schoolyard after the investigation, whether he thought they should be taken to Jacksonville and placed in jail overnight. The railroad official told Williams he thought they would be safe in town for the night if a sufficient guard was posted. He believed the talk about the Klan was just an attempt to scare the prisoners; the Klan would not try anything with so much activity in the town.

While Williams and deputy George Smith were trying to decide where they could hold the prisoners for the night, a member of the posse who had remained in Patona as a lookout for more suspects galloped up on horseback and told them he had seen one of the attackers return to his cabin. The deputy picked several men to go with the scout and bring the man, Jim Hughes, back for questioning.[16]

It was dark when the small party of white men tramped back to Patona for the third time in twenty-four hours, their tempers whetted by a sleepless night and their path lighted by sputtering torches. When the men entered the area near the water tower, called the "tank" by the local residents, a small boy darted by and was hauled into the light by one of the men.

"Whur're you going, boy?" a man asked.

"Goin' to tell Jim Hughes ya'll comin' to get him."

The boy's eyes were large with fear as he looked into the darkness behind the flickering torches.

"Who told you to do that, boy?"

The boy continued to gaze past them into the night. The iron grip of the man's hand closed tighter around the bare, black arm, and the boy's face twisted in pain.

Nabors pulled the man away.

"Who told you to do that, boy?" Joe Morrison leveled his pistol at the boy. Tears wet the dark, frightened face, and the boy's chin quivered.

"Joe!" Nabors cautioned.

"Mis'tuh Hall tole me to." The young voice was choked and weak.

82

"Hall," Morrison said sternly. "Which Hall?"[17]

William Hall was sitting on the front porch of his small cabin when the white men arrived and told him he was under arrest. When he asked them why they were arresting him, the scout told him it was because he tried to warn Jim Hughes, who had escaped.

Maria Hall sobbed loudly from the low porch as they took her husband away, then broke into a chilling wail that was heard all the way to the depot.

"If I don't see you no mo', take care of our chile," Hall called to his hysterical wife. And then they were gone.[18]

George Smith was alone at the school when the men returned with Hall. The sheriff had taken the other prisoners to the large porch of Nelson's new store near the crossroads for the night. The deputy walked with them down the street to the store and pointed the new prisoner to the long plank bench where Toney Cliff, Berry Harris, Caesar Frederick, and William Luke sat. Five of the men who were deputized to guard the prisoners stood around the platform as Smith talked with the posse.[19]

Hours earlier Klansmen had been seen among the curious, angry people at the schoolhouse. They had been highly visible since the beginning of the controversy, when villagers who belonged to the organization had been among the original defenders of the town. As the alarm spread into the countryside about the attack at Cross Plains, Klansmen had been the first to respond. Many of the men who joined the official posse belonged to one of the three dens in northeastern Calhoun County.[20]

These same Klansmen left the schoolhouse in anger when darkness came and the guilt of the captured prisoners was still undetermined by Slade Nabors and his "court." The attack by the gang of blacks infuriated the

Klansmen, and they stamped out of the schoolhouse, angry because Luke and the blacks would not be punished that night.

The Klansmen were apprehensive. They caucused in small groups around the schoolyard, debating what the next day's events at the court might bring. Some of the prisoners might be found innocent, and even if the blacks were guilty, the sheriff would take them to jail in Jacksonville. If that should occur, the Freedmen's Bureau or the federals could step in, and they might never come to justice.

Luke was the real plum in the eyes of the Klan. That afternoon in the schoolhouse Luke was thoroughly interrogated, not so much about his involvement in the attack but about the railroad school and what he was telling blacks around the county. All that was thought or rumored about the obscure Canadian was examined in the open forum of angry townspeople, misinformed outsiders, and the ever-present Klansmen.[21]

The Klansmen burned with a deep, passionate hatred for Luke. His fate was already decided; an execution squad had been selected. Sentiment was in their favor to consummate Luke's death, with the town in a turmoil, if they acted quickly.

As the milling crowd at the school began to drift back to their homes, still upset over the lingering excitement that had disrupted life in the village, the Klansmen had devised a scheme that would stigmatize the day in the history of the town. Klansmen were purposefully returning to their homes and communities, taking with them other Klansmen who had come to help the town earlier in the day.[22]

Their plan called for a rendezvous at the Baptist church by eleven o'clock that night, armed, in full regalia, and prepared to take the prisoners by whatever force was necessary.

At nine o'clock from atop Chimney Peak near Jacksonville, a distance of about eleven miles, a signal fire could be seen clearly in all directions. At ten o'clock in the headquarters office at Patona, armed Klansmen burst through the door and ordered the night clerk to wire the northbound train to stop at Blue Mountain until it received further orders. Across the countryside, in virtually every community, the hoofbeats of horses sounded through farmhouses that were opened to the cooling night breeze.

The uncommon sound of several riders together late at night brought people to their windows to see shadowy, ghoulish figures astride horses festooned like their riders. Some of those who were awakened by the sound of the horses also saw the signal fire on Chimney Peak. They knew the Klansmen were on their way to Cross Plains with their own verdict. The absence of the train, its shrill whistle as regular as the engineer's watch, would be remembered by still more people.[23]

Klansmen were gathering for the meeting at the Baptist church as the prisoners made themselves comfortable for the last night of their lives. There were close to forty Klansmen in the churchyard. While some watered their lathered animals in the creek beside the church, the den from Cherokee County galloped into the yard, their horses winded and blowing as they were reined to a halt.

On the way to the meeting they caught a black man on the road with a cloth sack slung over his shoulder. When the Klansmen questioned him, one of their group remembered the name he gave them—Essex Hendricks— as one of the attackers who was identified by the woman in Tobetown.[24]

Rather than carry Hendricks with them, the den leader took him off the main road to a secluded place near Frog Creek, a small tributary that emptied into Terrapin Creek. Hendricks was hanged and a volley of shot fired into his body.[25]

The execution of Essex Hendricks set the tone for a raid the Klansmen considered to be necessary and patriotic. If there was any reluctance about the severity of the night's exercise by any of the men who rode into the churchyard, it was dispelled by the action taken in Cherokee County. Cross Plains was not the place for the burning cross or the hickory withe. The Klan was forced into a more lethal course of action by the very nature of a crime that was distinctly southern—blacks revolting against whites.

After turning the prisoners over to the sheriff on Monday afternoon, Andrew Bailey discussed the facts briefly with the sheriff and the justice of the peace, and then he went home and slipped wearily into bed. By eleven-thirty the major was awake again, sorting out the sounds and the voices, the anger and the fear of the events that crowded into his mind since he was aroused from sleep the previous night. He understood the controversy as few people in the town did, and some of the things he had heard members of the posse say during the day troubled him. He had seen men with their faces twisted in anger and had heard voices—hard and demanding—making threats to the prisoners as they trooped back from Patona. When he left the schoolyard that afternoon, he saw these same men huddled together in conversation.[26]

Dressing quickly, Major Bailey started down the street toward the center of town. He had not gone far when he was conscious of movement behind him, not loud or

Cross Plains House, the hotel where William Luke had his last meal. Later named the Albert House. (*Piedmont Historical Society*)

alarming but a sensation of a presence. Bailey slipped into the shadows in time to see a large body of disguised Klansmen tread quietly down the street toward the center of town.

From the shadows of the houses along the street, Bailey followed them until the Klansmen came to the hotel and surrounded it. The moonlit night and the open street between the hotel and depot revealed more than sixty men, many in grotesque hats, sheathed in togas of white, yellow, and black, some more elaborate than others. A .44 caliber revolver, one of the more popular handguns of the day, seemed to be in the grasp of every man in front of the hotel; many of them had a pistol in each hand; a few of the pistols were cocked and at ready.[27]

As Major Bailey approached the throng of men, he

heard them making low, strange noises, guttural in tone, menacing the hotelkeeper, who was standing nervously on the front gallery. The keeper's voice quavered as he tried to convince the Klansmen that the prisoners were not at the hotel. When several Klansmen started up the steps to see for themselves, he pleaded with them not to go upstairs; they would frighten the ladies who were guests.[28]

Bailey moved through the crowd and mounted the steps to face the Klansmen. "They're not here," he told them. The hooded men demanded to know where the prisoners were being held; Bailey told them he did not know.

George Smith sat alertly on the front of the platform of Nelson's store most of the night, getting up periodically to stretch himself or to oversee the changing of the guards. Twelve men volunteered to stand watch with him; part of them guarded the prisoners while the others slept. At eleven o'clock the guards changed, each man handing over his pistol to one of the new guards coming on duty.[29]

The deputy did not hear the Klansmen padding down the street from the hotel some three hundred yards to the north. He suspected nothing until suddenly a small group, not more than fifteen, appeared around the platform.

Smith sprang to his feet, a hand on the revolver at his side. The deputy knew immediately what the intruders wanted. All the guards but one slipped away from their positions at the back of the platform when the Klansmen appeared at the front of the store. The single guard moved to the lawman's side and raised his pistol. Two Klansmen wrested the gun from his hand and pressed the heavy barrel of a dragoon revolver to the temple of the guard—all without speaking a word.[30]

A voice in the dark demanded the prisoners. A moment passed, a tense, hushed stalemate, before a shrill whistle was blown. The host of Klansmen surrounded the platform, appearing quietly and quickly out of the darkness, their bizarre costumes and their overwhelming numbers bringing the prisoners to their feet and evoking an audible groan from one of the blacks.

The low, strange noises started again, sounds not above a loud whisper, and the word "Lukie" was heard in an equally low tone from the mob.

In the meantime, Major Bailey left the hotel and began to follow the Klansmen. As he neared Nelson's store he saw them crowding the deputy and the prisoners into a tight circle. A smaller group of hooded men stood beside the store, busily cutting and measuring lengths of rope from a new coil that lay at their feet.

George Smith was earnestly trying to reason with the disguised men when Bailey forced his way through the Klansmen. The noises continued at random around the circle, but no one responded to the deputy's pleading.[31]

Major Bailey joined the deputy in his plea for the prisoners. He told them everything was being done to obtain justice in the shooting and the sheriff was searching for the other attackers. Bailey tried to assure them the authorities would handle the situation if given time. The major's words were lost in the night. One of the men standing behind him, an astronomer's hat duncing his head, said, "Shoo, fly."

The deputy's words had no effect on the masked mob. The Klansmen did not defend their intentions or even attempt to reply to either of the men. "Shoo, fly." The phrase was repeated again from another part of the crowd.

"Give the law more time," Bailey pleaded again. He

said, "I realize you believe you are doing the community a favor, but you are not. What you want to do with the prisoners will hurt the town."[32]

The Klansmen ignored Bailey and crowded closer to the prisoners, their pistols poised and aimed at the prisoners' heads. Before Bailey finished speaking they grabbed the five men and began putting ropes around the necks of three blacks. The deputy and the guard were forced off the platform and to the side of the store. Bailey was left standing alone, ignored like his pleas.

The only person to speak during the taking of the prisoners was William Luke. "I know I've done wrong, but I don't deserve this," he said as the Klansmen took him away.[33]

The prisoners were rushed off quickly—almost in a run—down the street and across the railroad tracks. The main body of the Klan followed behind them, several walking backward with their pistols leveled at Bailey and the deputy who appeared from beside the store as the mob left.

The guard who had not fled when the Klan appeared started down the street after them, but the men forming the rear guard thumbed back the hammers of their pistols and warned him to stop. The guard was left alone in the moonlit street, the mob lost in the darkness.[34]

The execution squad that took charge of the prisoners at Nelson's store hurried them up the main street to the edge of town. The Klan massed at the grove. The site had been selected for the hangings before the meeting at the church that night, primarily because of the oak trees and their heavy, accessible branches. Some of the Klansmen remained at the grove to watch the horses and stop anyone from entering the town.[35]

The coil of rope was not long enough for five nooses. The executioners solved the problem by hanging three of the blacks, then cutting two of them down and using the rope for the others.[36]

Torches were lit. The three black men with ropes around their necks were hanged first. While the first group of prisoners was being hanged, Luke asked for time to write a letter to his wife. He was given ten minutes. The mob of Klansmen milled about the grove as Luke took paper from his coat pocket and, with sure death only a few minutes away, composed his last letter to his wife.

Patona, Ala.
July 11, 1870

My Dear Wife;

I die tonight. It has been so determined by those who think I deserve it. God only knows I feel myself entirely innocent of the charge. I have only sought to educate the negro. I little thought when leaving you that we should thus part forever so far distant from each other. But God's will be done. He will be to you a husband better than I have been, and a father to our six little ones.

There is a balance of little over $200 in the company's hands of my money; also my trunk and clothes are here. You may send for these matters or let Henry come after them.

God of mercy bless and keep you ever dear, dear wife and children.

Your William[37]

The noise of the hangings interrupted Luke's thoughts as he wrote his last letter, especially when pistol shots administered the *coup de grace* for two of the suspended men. With the few minutes remaining after he finished the letter, Luke knelt in prayer until the executioners called for him.

The men were hesitant. The blacks were hanged quickly, but Luke was a white man, and the same enthusiasm did not urge them on. A strange awkwardness spoiled their moment of vindication.

The Klansmen did not want to hang Luke the same way they had hanged the blacks. The executioners decided to position a mule under one of the trees, rather than hang Luke from a standing position on the ground. They lifted Luke to the back of the mule. He sat there for a while, looking in resignation at his assassins until one of the Klansmen, a former Confederate soldier, stepped quickly into the circle of executioners, yelled loudly, and slapped the mule from behind.[38]

# X

# Aftermath of
# the Tragedy

✝ THE TOWN WAS ALIVE before dawn on Wednesday. The previous night Major Bailey and a small group of people had watched helplessly in front of Nelson's store as the Klan carried Luke and the blacks up the main street into the darkness. Their worst fears were realized when the sound of shots came from the north end of town. Later, after more townspeople rushed into the crossroads to investigate the excitement, the Klansmen returned, racing wildly down the street on their disguised horses, whooping and shouting. The Klansman who led the mob down the street on a chestnut horse yelled that they should ride to Patona.[1]

Even before dawn those who continued to maintain a vigil knew that the Klan was on the trail of Green Little. Later in the day news reached Cross Plains that they caught him at Pryor Station across the Georgia line. On the way back to Cross Plains, the Klansmen decided to hang him. Green Little thus became the seventh and last victim of the massacre.[2]

The trauma of the Klan's deed overwhelmed the town. People withdrew in shock and remained in their homes and places of business. Later in the morning Sheriff

Williams and his deputy, George Smith, conducted a coroner's inquest over the five victims. The verdict was that they had been hanged by unknown assailants.

Slade Nabors lived several miles out of town near Nancey's Creek and did not know about the hangings until the next morning when he arrived for the conclusion of the hearing. He rode out to the grove to see the murdered men.

Henry Brown, Judge Charles Pelham, and William Savery arrived around noontime with a wooden oxcart and a hastily built coffin. They did not tarry long. When the pine box was loaded on the sturdy cart, the three men left for Patona and the railroad offices.[3]

The next day, after the numbness subsided, a meeting was arranged by the more responsible citizens of the community to obtain some official perspective about the tregedy. At nine o'clock the Cross Plains Institute was again filled with townspeople. A committee was appointed to investigate the hangings. S. D. Johnson was elected chairman, and Leonidas Ferguson served as the recording secretary. Slade Nabors, H. A. Hayes, and Gilbert C. Craig made up the rest of the committee.[4]

The men spent all day assembling the facts for an official version of the hangings. It was little more than a continuation of Monday's investigation of the attack. The primary difference was addition of the testimony of the men who had witnessed the taking of the prisoners. The citizens quickly sifted through the evidence and agreed on satisfactory conclusions. The town felt itself to be aggrieved because the blacks had assaulted innocent women and children and the executions had come at the hands of outsiders—an organization that did not officially exist.

The initial appraisal of the committee portrayed the town as the victim of an attack by a group of marauding blacks and disclaimed any association with the mob of Klansmen. On Wednesday, 13 July, the committee issued two reports. The first was a full account of the hangings, beginning with the fight on the depot platform the previous Sunday night.

The second report was a series of resolutions that expressed the community's attitude toward the outrage:

> Resolved, that in the sense of this community, the forcible taking away of prisoners from the civil authorities in this town on the night of the 11th inst. by disguised persons is disapproved, and that we discontenuance any and all such proceedings believing them to be an injury to any community.
>
> Resolved, that the thanks of this entire community are due to our friends from the county generally. Especially those who came so promptly from Ball Play and Natville in such force to aid us in the protection of our property and the lives of our families. To them we tender our heart felt thanks and gratitude.
>
> Resolved, that in the opinion of this meeting, the magistrates, sheriffs and all the civil officers engaged, deserve the thanks of this community, for the prompt manner in which they discharged the duties imposed on them at the recent disturbances at this place.[5]

A member of the community, an elderly gentleman, caught the southbound train that afternoon and hand delivered the reports to Governor Smith the next day in Montgomery.

James F. Grant, publisher of the *Jacksonville Republican*, ran the resolutions and a lengthy article about the tragedy in the next issue. In his account of the outrage, Grant placed the blame exclusively on Luke's inflammatory racial attitudes. The editor closed the story by printing Luke's last letter to his wife. Summing up, Grant wrote:

The letter is a perfect model of ingenuity and shows the ruling passion strong in death to perfection. It was written to effect the popular mind at the North and it will effect well its purpose to the injury of the South. It is plainly implied in it that he was killed because he taught a negro school, and not one word is said of the charge that he incited the riot.

It is well known that he was one of the most rabid negro equality fanatics that ever came into this section, and the circumstances attending his misrepresentation of the people of Jacksonville to Gov. Smith and Gen. Crawford, and the attempt to embroil men of this place with the military are remembered by all.

He had repeatedly been advised by friends and warned by enemies to desist from the course he was pursuing, as it would inevitably lead to the results stated above.[6]

The hangings became a news sensation when a description of the outrage was printed in newspapers, first in Alabama and throughout the South and eventually across the nation. "Luke was a fanatic of the deepest dye and took a peculiar delight in arraying the Negroes against the people among whom he came to live," the *Rome* (Georgia) *Daily* (12 July 1870) stated. The *Montgomery State Journal* (16 July 1870) observed that "Glorious Old Calhoun has opened the Democratic campaign with murder," allowing the Democrats to use the incident with a telling effect in the 1870 state elections. The Cross Plains massacre became an event of national importance for the Republicans, who used it as a campaign item for the Radical cause.

"Luke and his dupes deserved death," the *Selma Southern Argus* (24 July 1870) opined. "They had attempted, and without provocation, assassination." The only paper in the state to carry an account worthy of being called impartial was the *Alabama Journal* in Montgomery.

Now that this unfortunate man has gone to his final reward, a determined and persistent effort is being made to blacken his character. Indefensible on any ground, his assassination is charged as the legitimate result of his own incendiary teachings. We are told by many who have known him long and well that a more inoffensive man lived not in all that region. Though firm and pronounced in his opinions, he never on any occasion sought to advance them by violence in deed or word. The only part he had taken in this affair was to endeavor to allay the anger of the negroes, and to prevent the party from going to Cross Plains.[7]

The Democratic papers portrayed the tragedy as the result of the racial problems caused by the intervention of the Radicals into local affairs. The Republican papers called it an example of Democratic justice, pointing out that "Old Secesh" was not fully dead in the South. And the North, always attendant to southern fault, reinforced longstanding beliefs of brutality and simmering rebellion with vivid descriptions of the multiple executions.[8]

Much of the blame for the Ku Klux atrocities was placed on Governor Smith for his failure to stem the tide of Klan violence. The Cross Plains hangings became coals of fire on Smith's head as he campaigned for re-election that fall, and he was constantly on the defensive about his efforts to contain the Klan. Robert Burns Lindsay, the Democratic nominee for governor, stumped the state accusing Smith and the Republicans of creating a reign of terror, naming the riots and the hangings as the product of Republican policy.[9]

"We understand that ex-Governor Parsons, was running around like a little dog at camp-meeting," the *Talladega Sun* reported, "trying to get up an 'indignation meeting' upon the arrival of the body of Luke." A group of Talladega officials left for Washington immediately to report the atrocity.[10]

William Smith arrived in Cross Plains by the end of the week with military and state officials, including General Samuel Crawford, to see what measures were being taken by county authorities to apprehend the killers. A squadron of cavalry under a Lieutenant Ulio reported on the scene on Thursday to take statements from Major Bailey, Slade Nabors, and others who were knowledgeable about the attack and the hangings.[11]

Intent on making an example of justice out of this most atrocious of all Klan acts in the state, the plump, black-bearded governor was conspicuous as he made his way around the village in a carriage, escorted by a blue-coated cavalry unit. By Sunday, a week following the events that triggered the tragedy, Cross Plains had become the object of intense interest from curiosity seekers who rode through town and visited the grove where the executions took place. Newspaper reporters from Montgomery were staying at the hotel and questioning people on the streets.[12] An interracial fight, a white man from Canada who taught black children, and a mob of disguised men who took justice upon themselves had suddenly pulled Cross Plains out of obscurity.

The town, which was perceived initially as the victim, lost its innocence when the Klan resolved the crisis of the prisoners' guilt with a sweeping declaration for white supremacy. Cross Plains was now categorized, not because the town had erred or because of a fault in judgment, but because of the folly of outsiders whose myopic concept of humanity did not include the Christian visionary or an unshackled race of people.[13]

"Harder than flint must be that heart which fails to bleed," a Montgomery paper lamented, "as he peruses the message of the husband and parent hurried to an untimely grave for such a cause." The editorial warned the perpetrators of the crime, "With what measure ye mete, it shall be measured unto you again." Another Montgomery source said the murders constituted one of the most aggravated and barbarous outrages that had ever disgraced the state.[14]

Governor Smith was interested in the crime for political reasons. The mass execution would further complicate a gubernatorial campaign that was going badly. He wanted to find a sensational way to apprehend the killers so as to enhance his reputation. He offered a $400 reward for "all information . . . respecting the movement of disguised men." The reward went unclaimed.

On the advice of the military and his personal staff, Smith contrived a dramatic plan to obtain justice and at the same time call attention to his official influence. He would arrange for an impressive, highly publicized investigation that would ferret out the guilty. By finding and successfully prosecuting the assassins, Smith would be able to stifle widespread criticism that he was allowing the Klan to run rampant over the state to prey on blacks and Republicans. One paper observed that the governor had "hurried from place to place" in preparation for the inquiry "and made his arrangements deliberately."[15]

Smith wired Lewis Parsons in Talladega and asked him to meet him in Patona. The next day in the railroad headquarters the governor met with Parsons, General Crawford, and the railroad officials to make plans for an extensive investigation. The men decided to conduct a court of inquiry with former Governor Parsons serving as the prosecuting attorney. The federal troops would be at his disposal to make the investigation as broad as necessary. The railroad offered space over the depot offices in Patona for the courtroom.[16]

When the governor returned to Montgomery he conferred with Thomas M. Peters, an associate justice of the Alabama Supreme Court, about the plan to hold an

Thomas M. Peters, associate justice of the Alabama Supreme Court. He presided over the court of inquiry at Patona. (*Alabama State Department of Archives and History*)

investigating court at Patona as a deterrent to more tragedies. The governor asked Peters to research the legal capacity of the court to intervene into local matters and to provide the state with the judicial authority to conduct the inquiry. He also asked Peters to act as presiding judge, promising him the freedom and the authority to make the investigation as effective as necessary to obtain evidence. Peters accepted and with Lewis Parsons's consent set 18 August as the date for the court to begin officially.

The governor had little choice other than to create his own system of justice. Since the local courts functioned ineffectively in cases involving the Klan, he knew the civil authorities would not pursue the investigation of the hangings earnestly. His court of inquiry, which would have the power to detain but not to convict, was designed to gather an overwhelming amount of information and turn the evidence and the guilty men over to the circuit court, forcing the county to return indictments against the killers.[17]

In the meantime, news of the atrocity continued to spread, reaping criticism for Governor Smith within the state and condemnation for the state elsewhere. By the time Peters and Parsons arrived in Patona, the beleaguered Smith was already promising prompt action for the mass lynchings in his campaign speeches, citing the impending investigation as a sure measure to help curb Klan violence in the state. The governor contended that fewer than fifty people had been assassinated since he took office two years previously. He argued that most Alabamians did not manifest "a lawless disposition."[18]

Captain Barney returned from New York and took a particular interest in the investigation. Above the offices in the depot was a small room with a sharply sloping ceiling that overlooked the large freight area below.

Barney had the room converted into a courtroom and consulted the sheriff about the items needed to furnish it properly.[19]

Although the investigation formally began three weeks after the hangings, it was not until Thursday, 18 August, that the court actually went into session. During the ten-day period before the opening of the court, the sheriff and Lieutenant Charles Hawkins, who was given command of the troops stationed in Patona, assembled the witnesses and took statements from them about the tragedy.

In giving Lieutenant Hawkins his orders, General Crawford specified the role of the military:

> When called upon by competent authority, you will furnish such a force mounted or foot as will be sufficient to accomplish the purpose requested, and they will accompany the sheriff and will execute his orders, and officers should accompany the posse to preserve order in the command; but in no case will he interpose unless called upon by the sheriff and his action will then be as one of the posse alone. You will not permit yourself or any of your officers to be deputized by the sheriff.
>
> You will be responsible for the safe-keeping of the prisoners entrusted to your care. Remember however that they are in the custody of the sheriff and that the military force used to guard and protect them is simply in aid of and to support his authority and not to supercede it.
>
> Keep your men well in hand and carefully avoid any just cause of complaint from the citizens, warning whom you may be thrown in the discharge of your duty.
>
> As far as desolves upon you, you will see that every comfort is supplied to the prisoners that may be placed in your charge, and you will forbid all communication with them during the night.[20]

On Thursday, when the court opened, Patona and Cross Plains were alive with activity. Judge Peters and former Governor Parsons arrived by the early train and were met by a squadron of cavalry commanded by General Crawford. Waiting inside the depot were several reporters, including one who filed his stories under the pen name "Carlos" for the *Cincinnati Daily Times*.[21]

William Bibb Figures, editor of the *Huntsville Advocate,* a Republican and a personal friend of Governor Smith, had a special interest in the court. Several days before the opening of the court, he published "Pen Portraits" of the men who would lead the investigation for the state.

In the personality profiles the editor revealed little-known facts about the men to impress his readers with their professional qualities. General Crawford was the holder of doctorates in both law and medicine; Lewis Parsons was a descendant of Jonathan Edwards, and Judge Peters was "one of our original Union men, 'to the manor born.'" All of these distinguished gentlemen were, according to Figures, integral parts of "the greatest and best government on earth."[22]

In the beginning of the investigation citizens of Cross Plains assumed a neutral position about the governor's court of inquiry. They favored exposing the lawless element that had blackened the town's name, but they could not bring themselves to cooperate with the hated Radicals. When the court opened, the atmosphere was positive and hopeful.

Whatever confidence the town had in the court was quickly lost. One of the first witnesses to be examined was Jacob Moore, the black whom the doctor had said would not live through the night of the lynchings. Moore had survived wounds that were not as bad as he pretended the night he lay on the bench in the schoolhouse. He feigned extreme pain, he told Judge Peters, because he was afraid he would be hanged if he went with the other prisoners. When Lewis Parsons asked him why he thought they were going to be hanged, Moore said that some of the posse had told them this would be their fate while taking them to Cross Plains the day of the examination.

In the safety of the court, Moore implicated three men who had been brutal and threatening in capturing the prisoners. He said Andrew Bailey had harassed and beaten several blacks when he led the posse into Patona; Milton Keith had wounded Caesar Frederick with a shotgun; and Pat Craig had told him the blacks would be hanged that night.[23]

When Craig and Keith were summoned to the court, no one was surprised because they had started the train of events with the fight at the depot. But the accusation of Major Bailey, the leading defender of the town and the man who had pleaded with the Klansmen for the lives of the prisoners, particularly the manner of his arrest, angered the townspeople. The sheriff and a squadron of cavalry went to Bailey's home in the dead of night to arrest him. Bailey's older sister, a fifty-four-year-old spinster who kept house for the family, met the soldiers at the door with a pistol and challenged their right to arrest her brother at that late hour. She told them he would surrender in the morning—which he did, after breakfast.[24]

Within days after the opening of the court, the town was further alienated by the arrest of the five guards who had fled when the Klansmen appeared at the store—*particeps criminis,* Lewis Parsons called them. The court interpreted the action of the guards as assenting to the hangings—failure to defend the prisoners—making them suspect of being Klanmembers or sympathizers. The names of George Dempsey, Milton Keith, Joseph

Morrison, George Stewart, and John Nabors were added to the growing list of suspects.[25]

By this time the town began to view the court as little more than a witch-hunt, uncertain and groping, another example of radicalism that continued to lay waste to the state. The people in Cross Plains and Calhoun County became hostile and uncooperative and hindered the investigation by remaining silent whenever they were asked for information. "They appear to know more than they are saying," Judge Peters wrote to the governor in Montgomery.[26]

From Jacksonville, James Grant stoked the fires of dissent through the *Republican*, the county's major newspaper. Grant taunted the court by reporting that it was closed to the public. Sheriff Williams countered this false charge with a letter declaring the court was accessible to the public. The courtroom was even moved from the small room upstairs to the large freight area to accommodate the large crowds that attended the sessions daily. The sheriff also noted that federal troops were making every effort to assist him in the investigation and allowing him full authority in making arrests and serving warrants.[27]

In September, Grant wrote that "the Patona trial drags its slow length along."

Nothing as far as we can learn, has been elicited which does, in any way, incriminate the men under arrest for the killing of Luke and his associates.

Judge Peters still presides and ex-Governor Parsons still conducts the investigation in that latitudinarian manner heretofore noticed. This lattitude was allowed under the ruling of the court, we suppose, to give the examination that range and turn desired by those who first set the machinery grinding.

And while speaking of this, it is but proper to place the responsibility of this most extraordinary and expensive proceeding where it belongs. And we should mention that ex-Governor Parsons is not officiating in the character of a volunteer attorney, he is regularly employed by Governor Smith. In Governor Smith rests the entire responsibility of the whole thing—the quasi-political cast given the investigation—the military paraphanalia—the length of time consumed in eliciting testimony not relevant to the case.[28]

The exposition of the Klan and its conspiratorial nature were as important to the court as the apprehension of the murderers. Lewis Parsons spent considerable time with the witnesses trying to obtain evidence of an organized conspiracy in the county.

Eli J. Woolum, operator of a hack service between Cross Plains and Chattanooga, testified that he had seen disguised men at various times along his route in northern Alabama. But he was unable to name anyone in the area as a Klan member.[29]

A Pleasant Gap farmer, William J. Cooper, volunteered to testify about the existence of the Klan in his community. When he returned home, a rumor was spread that he had been arrested for assault and attempted murder, thereby defaming him and damaging his reputation.[30]

William Powell of Cross Plains was harassed and threatened for having given anti-Klan testimony. A letter he wrote to Governor Smith in broken, misspelled English illustrated how difficult life was for a Union man:

> I take the oppertunity of addressing you with a few lines in regard to the condition of Calhoun County. I just arrived at home las night from Patona. Judge Peters and Governor Parsons has had me as a witness for the state

Lewis E. Parsons, former governor of Alabama. He was the prosecuting attorney at the court of inquiry at Patona. (*Alabama State Department of Archives and History*)

and the Klu Kluck that has not bin arested said that if I
testify they will kill me or their friends will do it. So I
fear that I will be bush whacked by the clan for tha made
a atact on my brother, James Powel the 8 day of May,
1870 on Sunday night and tha discharged 7 or 8 guns at
him and he returned the shot and the thursday following their was a berrian at Cross Plains and the reports
said that he was kild by a shot that he received on
Sunday night, and I persoom it was a fact and my
brother had to leave his home to keep them from killing
him. Tha made a rade on me about the 9 of Feb. 1870
and it is dangerious for me to stay at home to gether my
crop, and I hate to do murder but I will kill before I will
be kild.[31]

Parsons kept a separate copy of the testimony that
revealed anything important about the Klan organization
in the South. Much to the disgust of William H. Forney,
the eminent Jacksonville attorney who defended the
white men in court, Parsons's interest became political,
diverting the interest of the court to the general problem
of southern resistance to military Reconstruction.[32]

Politics was a major consideration at Patona for the
Republicans. Governor Smith sat in on the court whenever his campaign schedule brought him into northeastern Alabama, causing resentment among the white
population and excitement among the blacks who
loitered around the depot. On one visit Richard Busteed, a federal judge from New York who was later
impeached from the bench, accompanied Smith to the
court. Pompous and obnoxious, Busteed listened to the
testimony of a witness by the name of Woolf and observed loudly and arrogantly that he had found the
source of the trouble in Cross Plains—the people were
animals. Smith put Busteed on the next train to
Montgomery.[33]

While the trial was in progress, Governor Smith sent an emissary to Washington to apprise President Ulysses S. Grant of the state of affairs in Alabama and to answer the president's personal inquiry about the Cross Plains tragedy. Another associate justice of the Alabama Supreme Court, Benjamin Saffold, accompanied General Crawford to confer with Grant about Governor Smith's campaign to rid the state of the Ku Klux influence.[34]

In the meantime, the court was besieged by blacks offering to testify against the Klan. Although what most of them said did not relate to the lynchings, the court nevertheless was eager to hear them. One black woman described pathetically how the Klan had hanged her husband in front of their small son. Judge Peters repeatedly denied William Forney's objections to dismiss the testimony as not relevant to the case before the court.

Anthony Jones shocked the court when he told how Klan members had dragged him from his cabin and whipped him, while several others raped his wife. The same week, Aaron Jones described how he was beaten and shot by a party who raided his cabin on a plantation near Jacksonville. Blacks were not the only witnesses to implicate local people as Klansmen. A white boy, William Woodruff, identified William and Thomas Estes with the organization. The Estes brothers and other Klansmen whipped the Woodruff boy for reasons that were never made public. Woodruff's sister rescued him from the beating with a shotgun blast over the Klansmen's heads.[35]

William Woodruff told the court he had seen men go into the storehouse on William Estes's farm and emerge in Klan disguises. On the night of the mass murders he watched a host of white men make the ghoulish transformation in the storehouse and then ride toward the church by the creek.

Oliver Dukes, the black hotel employee who alerted the whites in Cross Plains about the ensuing attack on the white boys, told the court that he was in front of the hotel when the mob of Klansmen returned from the hangings. They galloped down the main street "under whip and spur." Dukes said he recognized the Estes brothers by their mounts and their shrill yell.[36]

Other witnesses verified the involvement of the Esteses, and the storehouse on the brothers' farm became prime evidence in the inquiry. The Estes brothers were detained with the other prisoners.

# X I

# Justice Denied

✝ THE FEDERAL TROOPS in Patona could do little
to restrain the rampaging Klan. The northern part
of Calhoun County continued to be a no-man's land,
where neither the terrorists nor the civil authorities were
able to contain the other. If anything, the Klan became
more innovative in its attempts to quell the investigation.
Even citizens with no personal interest in the controversy
deeply resented the parade of state officials who fre-
quented the court.[1]

Lewis Parsons and Thomas Peters were given rooms in
the residence of Captain Barney during the inquiry.
Neither man ventured far from Patona alone, and Judge
Peters consistently refused to make any statements outside the courtroom, fearful of personal consequences.[2]

"At Patona we saw the instruments of the infamous
inquisition," observed the editor of the *Selma Times*. "Parsons in his position as prosecuting attorney was to be
seen and Peters the immovable judge was visible." The
editor surmised that "the blue coats of the Yankee soldiers proved beyond a doubt that somebody was afraid to
remain at that place unprotected by Yankee bayonets."

"We would remind some of the parties who have been doing everything to render themselves obnoxious to the citizens of Calhoun County," the editor warned, "that the men who executed Luke and the negro outlaws still live and have not been arrested."[3]

The trauma of the inquisition at Patona—with all of its nuances of vindictiveness—was being sent North through the pen of the veteran reporter, Carlos. Although he wrote exclusively for the *Cincinnati Daily Times*, Carlos's articles were picked up by other northern papers. In a late September edition, positioned prominently on the front page between cables updating world news and Saturday's game of the Cincinnati Red Stockings, appeared the first "Letter from Alabama."

Accustomed to covering Klan tragedies, Carlos opened the article with a paradoxical impression of southern men. The young men of the South were compared to their counterparts of Paris's Left Bank, except that southern youths preferred to carry a quid of tobacco in their mouths instead of a rose. He thought their faces had a white, sodden look, which was the result of bad whiskey and even worse women. "Their souls are generally deformed and their breath always a pestilence. If their mouths are open they are taking in whiskey or letting out obscenity." Conversely, the reporter held southern gentlemen in high esteem. Generous, chivalrous, and free from pettiness, the true gentleman of the South "will not take compound interest; he will not steal. And not to do these is rare in Yankee land." Carlos regarded the Klan controversy with disbelief. He was appalled that the average southerner refused to acknowledge the existence of Ku Kluxism. In spite of overwhelming evidence to the contrary, some people in the South simply ignored the Klan—even its most cruel acts. Carlos cited the recent murder of the solicitor of

Greene County, Alabama, as an example. The tragedy occurred when a band of forty armed and masked men rode into Eutaw one day and assassinated the Republican officeholder in a hail of bullets while he screamed for help in his hotel room. No one went to his aid. "There are men in the South, many of them men without a creed or moral principle," Carlos wrote, "men humiliated and furious, who fear no laws human or divine."[4]

The reporter found a wealth of news for his readers during his month-long stay at Patona. The Klan was concentrating all of its energy and subversive imagination on the Republican court. The people around Cross Plains found the night arrests especially offensive. They fumed about the soldiers who roamed the countryside and served court papers or searched for witnesses in the nighttime. Everyone thought there was enough time during the day to conduct court business without the Yankees prowling at night.[5]

The cavalry under Lieutenant Hawkins's command became a visible tool of the court. Union soldiers took up positions around the depot when the court was in session, and they foraged for witnesses as far away as Randolph County, fifty miles to the south. Patrols clattered over the hard clay roads in Ladiga and Goshen, and they were seen regularly on the hilltop square in Jacksonville.[6]

The investigation by the Republican officials and the high profile of the federal troops rallied support for the Klan. During the investigation many people who previously disdained the hooded fraternity and its secret tactics became allies of its cause. When a newspaper reported that the court refused to allow one of the prisoners to visit his sick wife, sentiment swelled on behalf of the men. "There it was a guiltless man languished while a wife lay dying only two miles away," the *Montgomery*

*Weekly Mail* lamented, "denied the sight of him, denied a single word of endearment from his lips."[7]

Soon after the detention of the ten men, the Klan planned a raid on the railroad headquarters to rescue them. Klansmen stalked the railroad yards, waiting for an opportunity. But someone heard of the impending rescue, and the blue-coated soldiers lay in ambush for the Klan. The rescue effort was eventually abandoned.[8]

Northern employees of the railroad were also targeted for harassment during the investigation. The Klan sent word that it was going to shave their heads and "attend to them." Threatening notes adorned with Klan markings were secretively delivered to the depots in Patona and Jacksonville. The messages were the same: The depot will be burned when the troops leave.[9]

As discouraging as the violence and intimidation were, the officials of the examining court also labored under the burden of probable failure. The Democratic papers taunted Peters and Parsons by predicting the grand jury would never return a true bill against any of the defenders. The governor could investigate all he wanted, but in the end it would be the people of the county who would determine guilt.

"Governor Smith has carried forward his prominent part in this program," one Republican editor wrote. "That these men will not be punished is not his fault. He cannot create a sense of justice or manufacture the sentence for a community."[10]

After the hangings, the Selma, Rome, and Dalton Railroad encouraged the investigations and offered its facilities to the state. The Klan seethed in anger. Reprisals were quick. Trees were felled across the tracks and rocks toppled into the path of night trains. Shots were fired into the depot.

The Klan's activity was so intense that the general operation of the line was affected. Work crews were accompanied by armed guards, and occasionally a team of soldiers rode with the engineer on the night run between Cross Plains and Jacksonville. Because of the rash of accidents and threats, the company sharply curtailed its night schedule.[11]

During this period of intense harassment, the Klansmen around Cross Plains found another reason to be concerned about the Patona investigation. Lewis Force, a member of a Klan den in Cherokee County, appeared before the court and offered to testify against the organization.

Force turned against the Klan when a fellow member raped his twelve-year-old daughter and fellow Klansmen freed the rapist from the Cherokee County jail. When the distraught father heard of the investigation at Patona, he rode down and volunteered to testify. The man who raped his daughter boasted openly of lynching Luke. His name was Weaver.[12]

Force proved to be a wellspring of information. He implicated Weaver, who escaped before he could be apprehended by the sheriff, but, more important, he gave the court an internal view of the terrorist organization. Force testified that the objectives of the Klan were to wrest control of the state government from the Republican party and to keep blacks out of politics. The oath of loyalty required Klansmen to rescue members of the organization who were jailed. If they were called to testify against a fellow member, they were to respond with silence. The former Klansman also illustrated the recognition sign for the court and the collection of reporters—a bent forefinger in a shaking hand. Following Force's appearance, the Klan notified its members of a meeting by firing two rapid gunshots at sundown.[13]

The testimony of Lewis Force was quickly fed through telegraph wires to the northern public. The revelation of titillating Klan secrets became front page news that eventually was carried across the eastern part of the nation. Klansmen in northern Alabama squirmed in discomfort.

The most dramatic threat to the railroad came one night when the examining court had been in session for a month. Just after midnight as the up train was nearing Sulphur Springs five miles west of Patona, the yellow light of the Dayton steam engine picked up debris blocking the tracks. The engineer began to slow the train when a shot ricocheted through the metal cab. An off-duty ticket agent ducked behind the boiler.[14]

As the train slowed, Klansmen galloped out of the forest on either side of the tracks. The nerve-piercing screams of the fabled rebel charge sounded in the darkness. The engineer released the throttle of the wood-burning engine and braced himself on the metal floor. Miraculously, the heavy-wheeled machine jolted and rocked itself through the pile of timbers without derailing and picked up speed. The night riders, their red, yellow, and black costumes flapping wildly, thundered along the tracks with the train.

For a mile the chase continued. Shots were fired wildly into the air. Soon the engine regained its speed and headed for the railroad tracks at Patona. The brakeman in the last car told company officials later that two to three hundred Klansmen had chased the train.

In spite of the broad powers given to the court and the benefit of federal troops to enforce the daily directives of the court, little evidence was gathered in the weeks of intensive searching and questioning. Governor Smith placed reward notices in all of the newspapers in a thirty-mile radius of Cross Plains, but southerners—even in their poverty—would not betray their own.

"The proofs, thus far, are very meager," Judge Peters wrote to William Smith after six weeks of sifting through

116

the daily grind of testimony, and "I doubt whether they will be made much stronger by further effort."[15]

On 8 October, after failing to uncover any more conclusive evidence and continuously frustrated by the stubbornness of the county residents, Thomas Peters adjourned the court of examination *sine die*. The five guards who were detained by the court were released for lack of evidence. Four of the prisoners were bound over to the current term of the Calhoun County Circuit Court for the murder of Luke and the four black men: William Estes, Thomas Estes, Sanford Slayton, and Patrick Craig. Bond was set at $2,000. Andrew Bailey, Milton Keith, and Patrick Craig were charged with assault with intent to murder in the shooting of Jacob Moore and Caesar Frederick and held under $1,000 bond.[16]

"I am disgusted at being compelled to say that the Great Court of Investigation," Carlos stormed in his last article, "for which so many difficulties have been overcome, so many dangers incurred, and so much money expended has now adjourned." An hour after the men were set free, Carlos said "they were shooting pistols in the streets of Cross Plains. Solomon in all of his glory was not a raid like one of them! I have seen a drunken tribe of wild Indians behave with more decorum."[17]

The next week the grand jury considered the evidence turned over to it from the Patona investigation. A handwritten document over eight hundred pages in length, containing the testimony of 140 witnesses, was offered as proof against the men already on bail. The grand jury refused to return a bill of indictment against any of them. The only official action taken by the local courts in the Cross Plains tragedy was to return a charge of assault against Jacob Moore, the wily black man who was wounded and escaped the hanging tree by his wits, to testify against his assailants.[18]

The *Republican* chortled its delight in the next issue:

The Patona trial—Smith's election card—the scene of Parson's triumphs and Peter's debaucheries has "busted," shut up, quit keeping, played out.

Patona has sank back into her former insignificance and there is no more oppression within her borders.

The negro witnesses have left, there is nothing left save the recollection of their intimacy and confidential relations with some of the Radical "big boys" of the state.

To go and look at Patona now, one would not think it had been so lately honored with a two months tarry of Chief Justice Peters and barrister Parsons, much less the recipient of occasional flying visits from his excellency Governor Smith.[19]

Judge Thomas Peters wrote an opinion of the examining court, which William Figures published in late October in the *Huntsville Advocate*. Peters refused to acknowledge that the action of Craig and the Keiths in "fighting in the street with fire arms" could be defined "necessarily and purely as self-defense." He believed that the people of Cross Plains had exceeded the limits of self-defense by raiding Patona and Tobetown; in doing so, they became the aggressors.

As for the Klan, Peters said that "this county is infested by one of those secret organizations, the members of which prowl only at night in the most carefully prepared disguises, who excite consternation and terror wherever they are seen . . . they profess to come from the Moon and affect to talk very different English." The judge observed that "it seems that the Moon they inhabit is found at or near the storehouse of Mr. Estes, Ladiga."[20]

Judge Peters also questioned the validity of Major Bailey's manner of arresting the blacks at Patona. He noted that one of the witnesses had heard Bailey give the command to "shoot the damned niggers as they come, and the guns went pop, pop, pop," and that many black men were knocked down and beaten before almost the entire village was captured and carried to Cross Plains in the rudest manner possible. Peters deemed it a "very improper way to serve a warrant of arrest in a criminal prosecution. It was trespass by the mode of its performance. One may have the legal power to act but if it is abused he becomes the trespasser from the beginning." Peters concluded his opinion of the outrage by stating, "I am not prepared to say how far society may go in protecting itself. It doubtless retains all the rights of self-defense. But the forms of law cannot be invoked in order to give immunity to the stronger portion of a divided community, who chooses to assail the weaker portion. This would soon make brute force the law of the land."[21]

The court of inquiry adjourned in defeat. The white citizens of Calhoun County—with an unlikely accomplice, the Klan—had thrown up a solid front against the Republican investigators and the federal army. The white South had lost the war that followed secession, but it had won the political and guerrilla warfare of Reconstruction.

Southerners continued to prevail in the postwar struggle because blacks—as the Cross Plains hangings illustrated—were unable to defend themselves; because whites rebelled fiercely against the idea of racial equality; but eventually because they stubbornly wore down the will of the North.[22]

The memory of Reconstruction endured meaningfully among white southerners. Fact and fable immortalized for successive generations tragedies similar to the one born on the loading platform at the Cross Plains depot and reaching national prominence at another depot less than a mile away.

119

# Epilogue

✝ THE SENSATION created by the hangings in Cross
Plains did not end with the court of inquiry in October 1870. It became part of the larger issue of southern
resistance to Radical Reconstruction, a controversy that
was to continue through the 1870s until southern whites
regained control of state governments across the Old
Confederacy.

The Ku Klux Klan conspiracy became a major problem for the Republican party and its effort to redevelop
the South, prompting President Grant to address a special message to Congress in which he declared that the
"free exercise of franchise has by violence and intimidation been denied to citizens in several of the states lately
in rebellion."[1]

A select congressional committee was appointed from
the new Congress to investigate the political problems of
the southern states. Alabama Representative C. W. Buckley, a Radical and former minister for the Freedmen's
Bureau, was chosen to serve on the committee.

The committee met initially in Washington but later
that year began to travel to problem areas. It met in
Huntsville in October 1871, where Lewis Parsons,

William Forney, and others from the county gave their testimony about the Cross Plains hangings. In 1872 the committee published its findings in the *Report of the Joint Select Committee to Inquire into the Condition of Affairs in the Late Insurrectionary States*; the Alabama testimony was contained in three volumes.[2]

On 31 January 1871, Mrs. Fanny Ann Luke, widow of William McAdam Luke, filed suit for damages against Calhoun County in the circuit court. Her lawyer, Jasper N. Haney of Dallas County, cited the law passed by the Radical legislature making it possible for the next of kin to recover damages up to $5,000 from the county whenever persons were injured or murdered by parties in disguise.

"Under the law," the *Republican* admitted, "as it stands, the widow cannot fail to get a verdict for the amount provided she proves that her husband was killed by disguised men; and it will have to be collected out of the county by a levy of a special tax; but it will be hard to prove, we think, that Luke was killed by such men, as the Patona trial failed to discover anyone who witnessed the killing."[3]

In the fall of 1874, when the suit came to trial, a verdict for the county was found by the jury. Mrs. Luke's attorney appealed to the Alabama Supreme Court, where the judgment was reversed and the cause remanded back to the circuit court.

When the case came to trial again the following year, the county's attorney, William Forney, moved for a *non suit*, because the Ku Klux law of 1868 had been repealed by the new Democratic legislature. Again Haney asked the supreme court for its opinion, and Justice C. J. Brickell stated that the law had been unconditionally repealed the previous year, affirming the judgment of the circuit court.[4]

William H. Forney, Jacksonville attorney who was the defense attorney at the court of inquiry at Patona.

Neither Mrs. Luke nor any member of her family came to Alabama in concern with the suits against the county. Depositions and evidence were taken by a judge in Toronto, Ontario, and filed by Jasper Haney in the local court. John DeArman, the former Republican treasurer of Calhoun County, agreed to be responsible for the costs in the unsettled case and the appeals.

In time the community recognized that William Luke was innocent of inciting the riot, the most serious charge that brought about his death. Nevertheless, the people of Calhoun County believed Luke had been grossly undiplomatic and inconsiderate of the times in his efforts to aid black people.[5]

The Democrats won the state elections in the fall of 1870, using the race riots to slander the Republican rule in Alabama. In a strange turn of events, Governor Smith refused to allow the new governor to take office. Smith barricaded himself in his capital office with a small force of federal troops. For two weeks, until Smith could be persuaded to leave, Alabama had two governors.[6]

Federal troops remained in Patona for a year after the investigation. The soldiers occupied themselves with a game new to the South—baseball—the first ever played in Calhoun County.[7]

The Reverend Henry E. Brown left Talladega College in the early 1870s to become a traveling secretary for the YMCA; Thomas Peters ran for governor on the Republican ticket in 1876 and lost; and Andrew Bailey was appointed justice of the peace for Cross Plains by the governor to give the town civil authority.

The dream of making Patona an industrial center never materialized. The next stockholders' meeting was moved back to Selma, and the development of Patona as the headquarters for the Selma, Rome, and Dalton Railroad ended. The machine shops, which were scheduled to be moved to the new railroad town, remained in Selma until the company was purchased by the East Tennessee, Virginia, and Georgia Railroad.[8]

In 1882, the East Tennessee, Virginia, and Georgia listed Patona on a prospectus as having a population of six hundred people. "It has fine water-power, and considerable manufacturing. It is surrounded by good farming country, portions of which are still well wooded, but most of the timber has been cut and manufactured into charcoal for the neighboring furnaces." The company also noted that the old town of Cross Plains was situated nearby, "but the new railroad town of Patona has far outgrown it, so that the old town is being absorbed by the new."[9]

For a time after the tragedy Patona flourished. Its timber was cut and sold to the Woodstock Furnaces in Anniston, and the depot remained open until the Southern Railway System acquired the property.[10]

Cross Plains survived to dominate the northeastern region of the county. In January 1871, the village began incorporation procedures which gave the town official status and organization—shortcomings the tragedy had illustrated to the community the previous year.

In less than two decades, when there remained no fundamental conflict between the aspirations of the North and South, northern industrialists invested in the town, surveyed and mapped it, and in 1888 renamed it Piedmont.[11]

In 1910 the railroad property was sold to a local citizen for $10,000—and Patona became part of Alabama's history.[12]

# NOTES

## CHAPTER I

1. Walter Jones, *Geological Survey of Alabama* (University, Ala.: Wetumpka Printing Co., 1933), pp. 154–63.

2. Jesse Richardson, *Alabama Encyclopedia* (Northport, Ala.: American Southern Printing Co., 1965), pp. 354–56.

3. H. C. Nixon, *Lower Piedmont Country* (New York: Duell, Sloan and Pearce, 1946), p. 4.

4. Willis Brewer, *Alabama: Her History, Resources* (Montgomery: Barret and Brown, 1872), p. 151.

5. Jerry A. Daniel, "Map of Benton County, Alabama, 1852" (1975), Liles Memorial Library, Anniston, Ala.

6. Saffold Berney, *Handbook of Alabama* (Birmingham: Roberts and Son, 1892), index map.

7. Glover Moore, *A Calhoun County, Alabama, Boy in the 1860's* (reprint, Jackson: University of Mississippi Press, 1978), pp. 47–49; Brewer, *Alabama*, p. 152.

8. Lee Forney Crawford, *Forney Forever* (Birmingham: Commercial Printing Co., 1967), pp. 87, 105; *Ninth Census of the United States, 1870*, M593, Alabama, Calhoun County, Roll 5.

9. Moore, *Calhoun County Boy*, pp. 14, 19.

10. *Selma Times-Journal*, 20 June 1868. E. G. Barney reported that company trains were running between Jacksonville and Cross Plains, a distance of fifteen miles (W. D. Brown, *Report of the Railroad Commission* [Montgomery: Brown Printing Co., 1887], p. 58). The report stated that the Cross Plains depot was still on private property.

11. *Jacksonville Republican*, 25 June 1870. A. S. Johnson and J. N. Hoop were listed as the owners.

12. Ibid., 10 September 1870. Tuition varied from two to four dollars.

13. Robert Savage, *The Story of Piedmont* (Centre, Ala.: Stewart University Press, 1979), pp. 32, 33.

14. Ibid., p. 57.

15. *Ninth Census of the United States, 1870*, Calhoun County.

16. V. J. Esposito, *The West Point Atlas of the Civil War* (New York: Praeger, 1962), pp. 148–54; Ethel Armes, *The Story of Coal and Iron in Alabama* (Cambridge: The University Press, 1910), pp. 180–81; Rex Miller, *Croxton's Raid* (Fort Collins: Old Army Press, 1979), pp. 87–88.

## CHAPTER II

1. Bena Brown Scott, "Beginnings of Talladega College," 27 April 1937, Talladega College Archives, TC/Adm. 4/3/2.

2. "Recollections of Yancey B. Sims," n.d., Talladega College Archives, TC/Adm. 1/1/3.

3. H. E. Brown, "The Murder by Ku Klux of W. C. Luke," *American Missionary* 14 (October 1870): 235.

4. Alumni Records, Oberlin College Library, Oberlin, Ohio.

5. William H. Skaggs, *The Southern Oligarchy* (New York: Devin-Adair Co., 1924), p. 69; H. E. Brown to Rev. E. P. Smith, Talladega, 1 November 1869, American Missionary Association Papers, hereafter referred to as AMAP; Historical Library of the National Council, Young Men's Christian Association, New York.

6. Interview with J. Douglas Pelham, October 1980.

7. For the origin of the term *scalawag* and its meaning, see Sarah W. Wiggins, "What Is a Scalawag?" *Alabama Review* 25 (January 1972): 56–61.

8. E. Grace Jemison, *Historic Tales of Talladega* (Montgomery: Paragon Press, 1935), p. 293.

9. Sarah W. Wiggins, *The Scalawag in Alabama Politics, 1865–1881* (University of Alabama Press, 1977), pp. 90, 123, 128, 129, 131, 139, 144. This work portrays Alabama scalawags

more favorably than the stereotyped image of them as political opportunists.

10. "Report by Reverend Henry E. Brown," n.d., Talladega College Archives, TC/Adm. 1/1/3.

11. Brown, "Murder of Luke," p. 236; Mrs. H. E. Brown to Edwin C. Silsby, Oberlin, 14 July 1917, Talladega College Archives, TC/Adm. 1/1/3; Scott, "Beginnings."

12. *Jacksonville Republican*, 6 August 1870.

13. Brown, "Murder of Luke," p. 237; Mrs. H. E. Brown to E. C. Silsby, Lancing, 8 March 1882, Talladega College Archives, TC/Adm. 4/3/2.

14. A copy of the letter Luke wrote just before his death and the wording on his tombstone were recorded by the school at the time of the burial (Savery Library, Talladega College). The epitaph read: "William Luke. Born Tyrone, Ireland, Aug. 11, 1831. Departed this life at Cross Plains, Ala. July 11, 1870. 'Be thou faithful unto death, and I will give thee the crown of life.'"

## CHAPTER III

1. H. E. Brown to E. C. Silsby, Oberlin, 27 January 1917, Talladega College Archives, TC/Adm. 4/3/2.

2. Quotation in H. E. Brown to Rev. Erasmus Cravath, Talladega, 16 September 1873, AMAP; see also Phebe Sparhawk to Rev. E. M. Cravath, Talladega, 20 May 1870; E. M. Sparhawk to Rev. E. M. Cravath, Talladega, 20 May 1870; H. E. Brown to Rev. E. P. Smith, Talladega, 4 January 1868, all in AMAP; Paul Buck, *The Road to Reunion* (Boston: Little, Brown, 1937), pp. 68–99.

3. Brown to Cravath, 16 September 1873; "Tent Meetings in Alabama," *American Missionary* 21 (November 1873), p. 4.

4. Loren Schweninger, "The American Missionary Association and Northern Philanthropy in Reconstruction Alabama," *Alabama Historical Quarterly* 32 (Fall and Winter 1970): 129–

57; H. E. Brown to Rev. E. P. Smith, Talladega, 7 March 1870, AMAP.

5. Henry Brown's employment record, Library of the National Council, YMCA, New York. After leaving Talladega College, Rev. Brown was the first international committee secretary for colored work. He remained in that position for fifteen years.

6. Hodding Carter, *The Angry Scar* (Garden City: Doubleday, 1959), p. 195.

7. W. E. B. DuBois, "Reconstruction and Its Benefits," *American Historical Review* 15 (July 1920): 781–99; Juanita Williamson, *Our American Missionary Association Heritage* (New York: American Missionary Association, 1967), pp. 34–35; Christine Robinson, "The Founding and Chartering of Talladega College" (Senior paper, Talladega, 1949), p. 3.

8. Brown to Cravath, 16 September 1873; Charles Pelham to Rev. Brown, Talladega, 30 October 1869, AMAP. In this letter Judge Pelham said, "The benefits resulting from the establishment of this school are by no means confined to 'book learning,' but extend to the development of a higher standard of morality, than has hitherto been attained by colored people."

9. Library of the National Council, YMCA, New York.

10. Mrs. H. E. Brown to E. C. Silsby, Lancing, 8 March 1882, Talladega College Archives, TC/Adm. 4/3/2.

11. H. E. Brown, "The Murder by Ku Klux of W. C. Luke," *American Missionary* 14 (October 1870): 235; May Jewell to Rev. E. M. Cravath, Talladega, 20 September 1870, AMAP; Margaret H. Scott to Mrs. Cleo Mitchell Espy, Talladega, 12 November 1949, Library of the National Council, YMCA, New York.

12. Henry E. Brown to E. C. Silsby, Oberlin, 27 January 1917, Talladega College Archives, TC/Adm. 4/3/2.

13. Brown, "Murder of Luke," p. 236.

14. Quotation in ibid., p. 235; see also Brown to Silsby, 8 March 1882.

## CHAPTER IV

1. Canada West Census, 1861. Part of the material on Luke's Canadian history was developed by Glenn Lucas and his staff

at the United Church of Canada Archives, Victoria University, Toronto, Canada.

2. *A Brief Historical Review of Annesley United Church, Markdale, Ontario, Canada, 1850–1950*, One Hundred Anniversary, 5 November 1950.

3. John Carrol, *Cyclopedia of Methodism in Canada* (Toronto, 1881), p. 114.

4. Deposition of Fanny Ann Luke, Circuit Court, Fall Term 1874, Alabama Supreme Court Records, Alabama Archives, Montgomery.

5. Canada West Census, 1861; Minutes of the Third Annual Meeting of the Ministers and Preachers of the Niagara District of the Wesleyan Methodist Church in Canada—St. Catherines, Wednesday, 31 May 1862, United Church of Canada Archives, Victoria University, Toronto. The Wesleyan Methodist church in Canada was directly connected to the original Methodist church in England.

6. *Christian Guardian* (published under the direction of the Conference of the Wesleyan Methodist church in Canada), 29 December 1858, p. 258.

7. Minutes of the 1862 Meeting of the Niagara District.

8. Carrol, *Cyclopedia of Methodism*, p. 114.

9. *Christian Guardian*, 31 December 1862.

10. Minutes of the Pontiac District of the Wesleyan Methodist Church in Pembroke, May 1864, United Church of Canada Archives.

11. Minutes of the Annual Conference at Elm Street Church in Toronto, 2 June 1864, United Church of Canada Archives.

12. Deposition of Rev. William Irwin, Circuit Court, Fall Term, 1874, Alabama Supreme Court Records, Alabama Archives.

13. H. E. Brown, "The Murder by Ku Klux of W. C. Luke," *American Missionary* 14 (October 1870): 237.

14. Walter L. Fleming, *The Reconstruction of the Seceded States* (Spartanburg: Reprint Co., 1978), p. 150.

## CHAPTER V

1. *Jacksonville Republican*, 14 March 1870; Thomas Fister to Gen. S. W. Crawford, 14 March 1870; J. L. Pennington to Gov.

W. H. Smith, Jacksonville, 31 May 1870, both in Governor's Correspondence, Alabama Archives. Attorney William Forney countered the many complaints by writing to Governor Smith: "The good citizens of this county will not only exert their energies in favor of preserving order and enforcing law, but will promptly aid the civil authority in executing legal process when called upon" (6 June 1870, ibid.).

2. Letters to Gov. Smith from W. P. Crook et al., Jacksonville, 13 May 1870, Governor's Correspondence, Alabama Archives.

3. Allen Trelease, *White Terror* (New York: Harper & Row, 1971), pp. 262–64.

4. Walter L. Fleming, *The Reconstruction of the Seceded States* (Spartanburg: Reprint Co., 1978); Sarah Woolfolk Wiggins, "Alabama: Democratic Bulldozing and Republican Folly," in Otto H. Olsen, *Reconstruction and Redemption in the South* (Baton Rouge: Louisiana State University Press, 1980), pp. 54, 56.

5. *Jacksonville Republican*, 8 April 1870.

6. E. G. Barney to Gen. A. H. Terry, Patona, 16 May 1870, Governor's Correspondence, Alabama Archives.

7. James F. Decamp to Gov. Smith, Patona, 29 June 1870, ibid.

8. J. N. Brown to Rev. E. M. Cravath, Talladega, 19 September 1870, AMAP. Justus N. Brown was Henry Brown's brother, who taught at the college for about two years.

9. Mrs. H. E. Brown to E. C. Silsby, Lancing, 8 March 1882, Talladega College Archives, TC/Adm. 4/3/2.

10. May Jewell to Rev. E. M. Cravath, Talladega, 20 September 1870, AMAP.

11. Brown to Cravath, 19 September 1870.

## CHAPTER VI

1. Mrs. H. E. Brown to E. C. Silsby, Lancing, 8 March 1881, Talladega College Archives, TC/Adm. 4/3/2.

2. Minute Books of the Selma, Rome, and Dalton Railroad, New York, 4 January 1869, Birmingham Public Library, Birmingham, Ala.

3. E. G. Barney to Gen. A. H. Terry, Patona, 16 May 1870, Governor's Correspondence, Alabama Archives.

4. H. E. Brown to Rev. E. P. Smith, Talladega, 1 November 1869, AMAP.

5. Brown to Silsby, 8 March 1882.

6. E. G. Barney to F. H. Delano, Avoca, 1 February 1869, Franklin Delano Roosevelt Library, Hyde Park, N.Y. Patona was originally named Avoca.

7. Brown to Smith, 1 November 1869.

8. H. E. Brown, "The Murder by Ku Klux of W. C. Luke," *American Missionary* 14 (October 1870): 236.

9. Brown to Smith, 1 November 1869.

10. Minute Books of the Selma, Rome, and Dalton Railroad, New York, 4 June 1868, Birmingham Public Library, Birmingham, Ala.

11. Ibid.

12. Ibid., 3 June 1868.

13. Information on E. G. Barney supplied by Miami County Library, Miami, Ohio.

14. E. G. Barney to Gov. William H. Smith, Patona, 1 June 1870 (telegram), Governor's Correspondence, Alabama Archives.

15. Brown to Smith, 1 November 1869.

16. Brown, "Murder of Luke," p. 236.

17. H. E. Brown's employment record, Library of the National Council, YMCA, New York.

18. W. C. Luke to E. G. Barney, Patona, 29 March 1870, Piedmont City Library, Piedmont, Ala.

19. William Luke to Fanny Ann Luke, Patona, 5 December 1869, *Fanny Ann Luke* v. *Calhoun County*, 1875, Alabama State Supreme Court Records, Alabama Archives, Montgomery.

20. William Luke to Fanny Ann Luke, Patona, Christmas Day 1869, ibid.

21. William Luke to Fanny Ann Luke, Patona, 28 January 1870, ibid.

22. Luke to Barney, 29 March 1870.
23. Brown to Silsby, 8 March 1881.
24. Luke to Barney, 29 March 1870; Brown, "Murder of Luke," p. 237.


CHAPTER VII

1. *Jacksonville Republican*, 13 March 1869.
2. Deposition of Edward Goode, *Fanny Ann Luke* v. *Calhoun County*, Alabama Supreme Court Records, 1875, Alabama Archives.
3. W. C. Luke to E. G. Barney, Patona, 29 March 1870, Piedmont City Library, Piedmont, Ala.
4. *Fanny Ann Luke* v. *Calhoun County*, Alabama Supreme Court Records; *Alabama Reports, 1875*, 12 (Tuscaloosa: M. D. J. Slade, 1878), 115–22; *Alabama Reports, 1876*, 56 (Montgomery: Joel White, 1879), 415–17.
5. Luke to Barney, 29 March 1870.
6. *Jacksonville Republican*, 6 August 1870.
7. Luke to Barney, 29 March 1870.
8. Ibid.
9. E. G. Barney to F. H. Delano, Avoca, 1 February 1869, Franklin Delano Roosevelt Library, Hyde Park, N.Y.; H. E. Brown to Rev. E. P. Smith, Talladega, 1 November 1869, AMAP.
10. Minute Books, Selma, Rome, and Dalton Railroad, 6 May, 9 June 1870, Birmingham Public Library, Birmingham, Ala.
11. *Jacksonville Republican*, 12 June 1870; Lucy Kavaler, *The Astors* (New York: Dodd, Mead & Co., 1966), pp. 54–55, 83. Franklin Hughes Delano was described as handsome; he occupied himself by looking after the affairs of his in-laws. He was married to Laura Astor, daughter of William B. Astor.
12. Minute Books, Selma, Rome, and Dalton Railroad, 9 June 1870.
13. *Jacksonville Republican*, 12 June 1870.

14. *Birmingham Age-Herald*, 21 October 1910.
15. *Jacksonville Republican*, 12 June 1870.
16. H. E. Brown, "The Murder by Ku Klux of W. C. Luke," *American Missionary* 14 (October 1870): 235–37.

## CHAPTER VIII

1. "A Report Supplied by Rev. H. E. Brown," Talladega College Archives, TC/Adm. 4/3/2; E. G. Barney to Gen. A. H. Terry, Patona, 16 May 1870, Governor's Correspondence, Alabama Archives.
2. J. W. Williams to W. H. Smith, Jacksonville, 12 July 1870, Governor's Correspondence, Alabama Archives.
3. Mrs. H. E. Brown to E. C. Silsby, Lancing, 8 March 1882, Talladega College Archives, TC/Adm. 4/3/2.
4. *Rome Daily*, 11 July 1870.
5. W. E. Studdard to Jack D. Boozer, Piedmont, n.d. (1960). The original is in the possession of Boozer.
6. Interview with Frank Little, Alexandria, Ala., October 1980. Little's grandfather, William Washington Little, was a member of the secession legislature from Cherokee County. Little was also the symbolic head of the Ku Klux Klan dens in the Goshen and Ladiga communities. His age—fifty-seven—kept him from accompanying the Klan on raids.
7. *Report of the Joint Select Committee to Inquire into the Condition of Affairs in the Late Insurrectionary States* (Washington: Government Printing Office, 1872), pp. 429, 468–69. The Alabama testimony is contained in volumes 8, 9, and 10. This work is referred to hereafter as Alabama Testimony.
8. Interview with Frank Little. Green Little acquired a reputation for being quarrelsome after gaining his freedom.
9. Alabama Testimony, p. 468; *Selma Press*, 23 July 1870.
10. *Cincinnati Daily Times*, 4 October 1870; Alabama Testimony, p. 468.
11. Alabama Testimony, p. 1238.
12. Ibid.

13. "Report of the Committee," 13 July 1870, Governor's Correspondence, Alabama Archives; Alabama Testimony, p. 1238.

14. Alabama Testimony, p. 469.

15. *Cincinnati Daily Times*, 4 October 1870; *Jacksonville Republican*, 6 August 1870; Alabama Testimony, pp. 469, 481, 482.

16. *Jacksonville Republican*, 14 July 1870; Alabama Testimony, pp. 469–70.

17. W. H. Smith to Gen. A. H. Terry, Montgomery, 22 July 1870, Governor's Correspondence, Alabama Archives.

18. Alabama Testimony, pp. 445, 469, 1236. The statement of A. D. Bailey was taken by Lieutenant Ulio of the Union army, 19 July 1870 and given in evidence to the select committee that convened in Huntsville in October 1871.

19. Interview with Frank Little; Alabama Testimony, p. 469.

20. Williams to Smith, 12 July 1870; Alabama Testimony, pp. 469, 1236.

21. Alabama Testimony, p. 1236.

22. *Huntsville Advocate*, 28 October 1870. This is the official opinion of Judge Thomas M. Peters (Alabama Testimony, p. 1236).

23. Alabama Testimony, p. 469.

24. Ibid., pp. 63, 470, 1236.

25. Ibid., p. 470.

26. *Huntsville Advocate*, 28 October 1870.

27. Alabama Testimony, pp. 470, 1236.

## CHAPTER IX

1. Alabama Testimony, pp. 63, 470, 1237.

2. Ibid., pp. 61–65, 428–85, 1235–36. Although minutes of the informal hearing were never printed, a remarkable account of the proceedings was preserved in the evidence given to the visiting select committee in Huntsville.

3. *Selma Press,* 23 July 1870; *Rome Daily,* 11 July 1870; W. H. Smith to Gen. A. H. Terry, Montgomery, 22 July 1870, Governor's Correspondence, Alabama Archives; *Piedmont Journal,* 28 September, 5, 12, 19, 26 October, 2, 9 November 1972.

4. Alabama Testimony, pp. 470, 446–47; *Rome Daily,* 12 July 1870.

5. *Jacksonville Republican,* 6 August 1870; *Selma Press,* 23 July 1870.

6. Alabama Testimony, pp. 446, 471; *Cincinnati Daily Times,* 4 October 1870.

7. Alabama Testimony, p. 471.

8. *Jacksonville Republican,* 6 August 1870.

9. W. C. Luke to E. G. Barney, Patona, 29 March 1870, Piedmont City Library, Piedmont, Ala.; Peter Kolchin, *First Freedom* (Westport, Conn.: Greenwood Press, 1972), p. 21. The migration of black laborers made it difficult for some areas in the South to obtain farm labor (*Jacksonville Republican,* 13 March 1869). The Calhoun County Agricultural Society acknowledged the labor problem and advised its members about handling the manpower shortage.

10. Alabama Testimony, p. 429.

11. *Jacksonville Republican,* 6 August 1870.

12. Alabama Testimony, pp. 63, 471.

13. Ibid., p. 470; Allen Trelease, *White Terror* (New York: Harper & Row, 1971), pp. 269–70.

14. Alabama Testimony, p. 63.

15. Ibid., pp. 446, 470, 471.

16. Ibid., pp. 63, 470.

17. *Huntsville Advocate,* 28 October 1870. Judge Peters's official opinion contained an account of "Little Pete's" brush with the posse.

18. Alabama Testimony, p. 63.

19. Ibid., p. 470.

20. *Huntsville Advocate,* 28 October 1870.

21. Alabama Testimony, p. 485.

*22. Interview with Frank Little, Alexandria, Ala., October 1980.

23. Alabama Testimony, pp. 446, 485.

24. Ibid., p. 472.
25. Interview with Frank Little.
26. Alabama Testimony, p. 1237.
27. Ibid., pp. 471, 485.
28. Ibid., pp. 473, 1237.
29. Ibid., p. 1237.
30. Ibid., p. 445.
31. Ibid., p. 1237.
32. Ibid., pp 471, 1237.
33. Ibid., p. 484.
34. Ibid., p. 473.
35. Interview with Frank Little.
36. Alabama Testimony, p. 429.
37. A copy of the letter made by H. E. Brown when he recovered Luke's body is in Savery Library, Talladega College.
38. Interview with Frank Little. Two other Klan outrages are prominent in Alabama history. In 1870 a rally for Republican Charles Hayes's reelection to the House of Representatives turned into a riot when Klansmen fired into a crowd of some two thousand blacks in Eutaw. Fifty-four blacks were wounded, four of them mortally (Trelease, *White Terror*, pp. 262–63; Alabama Testimony, pp. 466–67). In Huntsville the 1868 election was the scene of another Klan tragedy. One hundred fifty Klansmen rode into a Republican rally and rode out without any violence. As they were leaving, shots were fired indiscriminately and a minor riot broke out. Two people were killed and numerous others of both races wounded (E. C. Betts, *Historic Huntsville* [Birmingham: Southern University Press, 1920], pp. 114–19).

## CHAPTER X

1. *Rome Daily*, 11 July 1870; Alabama Testimony, pp. 467, 472.
2. Bena Brown Scott, "Beginnings of Talladega College," 27 April 1937, Talladega College Archives, TC/Adm. 4/3/2;

Deposition of George Smith and Slade Nabors, Alabama Supreme Court Records, Alabama Archives.

3. *Jacksonville Republican*, 14 July 1870.

4. "Report of the Committee," Governor's Correspondence, Alabama Archives; *Jacksonville Republican*, 14 July 1870; Alabama Testimony, p. 473.

5. *Jacksonville Republican*, 23 July 1870.

6. *Rome Daily*, 17 July 1870; Jack D. Boozer, "So Far Distant," Jacksonville, n.d. For years Boozer collected material on the Cross Plains tragedy, with the intent of writing a book about the sensation. Some of his material was used as a source in this work.

7. *Alabama Journal* (Montgomery), 21 July 1870.

8. *Huntsville Advocate*, 14 September 1870.

9. *Jacksonville Republican*, 23 July 1870.

10. *Talladega Sun*, 14 July 1870.

11. Alabama Testimony, p. 1236; *Jacksonville Republican*, 2 July 1870.

12. *Selma Times and Messenger*, 24 August 1870.

13. *Talladega Watchtower*, 20 July 1870.

14. *Montgomery Weekly State Journal*, 22 July 1870; *Monthly Report*, Supreme Court of Alabama, 18 July 1870.

15. *Selma Times and Messenger*, 24 August 1870; *Jacksonville Republican*, 30 July 1870.

16. J. W. Williams to Gov. Smith, Patona, 25 August 1870, Governor's Correspondence, Alabama Archives.

17. *Huntsville Advocate*, 28 October 1870.

18. *Jacksonville Republican*, 23 July 1870; W. H. Smith to Gen. Alfred H. Terry, Montgomery, 22 July 1870, Governor's Correspondence, Alabama Archives.

19. *Montgomery Weekly Mail*, 19 October 1870.

20. Gen. S. W. Crawford to Lieutenant Charles Hawkins, Patona, 11 August 1870, Governor's Correspondence, Alabama Archives; *Alabama Journal* (Montgomery), 26 August 1870.

21. *Cincinnati Daily Times*, 26 September 1870.

22. *Huntsville Advocate*, 21 August 1870; D. L. Dalton to H. L. Stevenson, Montgomery, 24 September 1870, Governor's Cor-

respondence, Alabama Archives. H. L. Stevenson was the young solicitor for Calhoun County who served as the clerk for the court of examination.

23. *Huntsville Advocate*, 28 October 1870; Alabama Testimony, p. 63.

24. Interview with Frank Little, Alexandria, Ala., October 1980.

25. Alabama Testimony, p. 471.

26. Thomas Peters to Gov. Smith, Patona, 20 September 1870, Governor's Correspondence, Alabama Archives.

27. Williams to Smith, 25 August 1870.

28. *Jacksonville Republican*, 18 September 1870.

29. *Huntsville Advocate*, 28 October 1870.

30. W. J. Cooper to Governor Smith, Pleasant Gap, 21 October 1870, Governor's Correspondence, Alabama Archives.

31. William Powell to Gov. Smith, Patona, 25 September 1870, Governor's Correspondence, Alabama Archives.

32. Alabama Testimony, p. 64.

33. Ibid., p. 467.

34. W. H. Smith to Gen. Alfred H. Terry, Montgomery, 26 July 1870, Governor's Correspondence, Alabama Archives.

35. *Huntsville Advocate*, 28 October 1870.

36. Alabama Testimony, p. 473.


CHAPTER XI

1. J. N. Brown to Rev. E. M. Cravath, Talladega, 19 September 1870, AMAP.

2. *Huntsville Advocate*, 14 September 1870.

3. *Selma Times*, 24 September 1870.

4. *Cincinnati Daily Times*, 22 September, 4, 10, 19 October 1870.

5. *Jacksonville Republican*, 18 August 1870. The *Cincinnati Daily Times*, 10 October 1870, reported: "Night arrests are

uncalled for, since parties arrested could have been had in court any day by intimation that their presence was desired."

6. Alabama Testimony, pp. 466, 473.

7. *Montgomery Weekly Mail*, 19 October 1870; *Jacksonville Republican*, 1 October 1870.

8. *Cincinnati Daily Times*, 10 October 1870.

9. Ibid., 4 October 1870.

10. *Huntsville Advocate*, 17 October 1870.

11. *Cincinnati Daily Times*, 10 October 1870.

12. Alabama Testimony, pp. 466–67, 471–74.

13. *Cincinnati Daily Times*, 10 October 1870; *Huntsville Advocate*, 11 November 1870.

14. *Cincinnati Daily Times*, 10 October 1870.

15. Thomas M. Peters to William H. Smith, Patona, 10 October 1870, Governor's Correspondence, Alabama Archives.

16. Alabama Testimony, p. 471; *Huntsville Advocate*, 28 October 1870.

17. *Cincinnati Daily Times*, 17 October 1870.

18. Alabama Testimony, p. 64.

19. *Jacksonville Republican*, 15 October 1870; *Montgomery Weekly Mail*, 19 October 1870.

20. *Huntsville Advocate*, 28 October 1870; Peters to Smith, 10 October 1870.

21. *Huntsville Advocate*, 28 October 1870.

22. Otto H. Olsen, *Reconstruction and Redemption in the South* (Baton Rouge: Louisiana State University Press, 1980), p. 230.

## EPILOGUE

1. Hodding Carter, *The Angry Scar* (Garden City: Doubleday, 1959), p. 216; John Hope Franklin, *Reconstruction: After the Civil War* (Chicago: University of Chicago Press, 1969), pp. 152–53.

2. Robert S. Henry, *The Story of Reconstruction* (New York: Grosset & Dunlap, 1938), pp. 437–39.

3. *Jacksonville Republican*, 6 February 1871.

4. The first suit was during the fall term (23 October) 1874 (Circuit Court Minutes, Calhoun County, Book F, Calhoun County Courthouse). The appeal is in *Alabama Reports, 1875,* 12 (Tuscaloosa: M. D. J. Slade, 1878), 115–22. The second suit was during the fall term (19 October) 1875 (Circuit Court Records, Calhoun County); the appeal is in *Alabama Reports, 1876,* 56 (Montgomery: Joel White, 1879), 415–17.

5. Edwin C. Silsby wrote to J. C. Williams, Talladega, 25 September 1919: "It was said of him [Luke] that he was not diplomatic and soon got the animosity of the lawless element of the town against him" (Talladega College Archives). Another account stated: "According to some authorities, the inception of the notorious Patona riots was one of the evil results of incendiary speeches made in that church. A notorious carpet-bagger named Luke, who was among those who were hung at Patona had made speeches in the Negro Baptist Church on Battle Street" ("Index to the History of Talladega, William H. Skaggs, Mayor," William Henry Skaggs Papers, Alabama Archives).

6. Henry, *Story of Reconstruction*, pp. 417–18.

7. Jack D. Boozer, "So Far Distant," Jacksonville, n.d.

8. Minute Books of the Selma, Rome, and Dalton Railroad Company, 16 May 1871, Birmingham Public Library, Birmingham, Ala.

9. Prospectus of the East Alabama, Virginia, and Georgia Railroad, in possession of Frank M. Jones, Birmingham.

10. S. M. Fry to George Noble, Patona, 28 May 1870, Piedmont City Library, Piedmont, Ala.

11. Robert Savage, *The Story of Piedmont* (Centre: Stewart University Press, 1979), p. 17.

12. *Birmingham Age-Herald*, 21 October 1910. This extensive article by Col. Harry Ayers, editor of the *Anniston Star,* tells the story of Patona and the dream of its founders. Details are also available in the Bessie Coleman Robinson Collection, Liles Memorial Library, Anniston, Ala.

# BIBLIOGRAPHICAL NOTE

## MANUSCRIPTS, UNPUBLISHED MATERIAL, AND NEWSPAPERS

Resource material about the Cross Plains hangings is widely scattered and for the most part unorganized. The Piedmont City Library in Piedmont, Alabama, maintains a cursory file about the tragedy and has extensive genealogical information about many of the people involved in the sensation. The primary historical document about the city was written by Robert Savage, *The Story of Piedmont* (Centre, Ala.: Stewart University Press, 1979). Mrs. Frank Ross Stewart collected much of the material about the lynching that appears in Savage's work. Mrs. Stewart also wrote *Alabama's Calhoun County* (Centre, Ala.: Stewart University Press, 1976), which included a section on Cross Plains.

Lane Weatherbee, editor of the *Piedmont Journal,* published a series of articles entitled "I Die Tonight" about the William Luke incident from September to November 1972. Most of the material for the articles was developed by Calhoun County historian Jack Boozer.

The most valuable personal account of the Luke hanging came from interviews with Frank J. Little, a grandson of W. W. Little, a participant in the Luke tragedy. The Bessie Coleman Robinson Papers in the Liles Memorial Library in Anniston also aided in the research about the town of Patona and the hangings. A reliable account of the lynchings and the aftermath was reported in the *Jacksonville Republican,* the most widely read newspaper in Calhoun County during Reconstruction. Jacksonville State University in Jacksonville, Ala-

bama, has a nearly complete collection of the paper. J. Douglas
Pelham of Anniston was interviewed concerning the Pelham
family during the period.

The Savery Library and Archives at Talladega College has a
wealth of information about the founding of the college during Reconstruction. The college archives maintains the most
extensive and best organized collection of documents about
William Luke in the state. The school also has the Edwin
Silsby Papers containing other material important to the Luke
incident. The research was supplemented by the American
Missionary Association Archives at Dillard University in New
Orleans. The more relevant information at the AMA was the
correspondence of association personnel during the founding
of the college. The historical library of the YMCA in New York
has a record of Henry Edwards Brown's employment with the
organization, and Oberlin College Library, Oberlin, Ohio,
maintained a file on Brown from his college days until his
death.

The Alabama State Department of Archives and History in
Montgomery houses a number of manuscripts relevant to this
period. The papers of William H. Smith, John W. Dubose,
Robert McKee, and Lewis E. Parsons were read for clues to
the Cross Plains sensation. The letters of Secretary of State
Charles Miller and Governor William H. Smith were also read
for pertinent material. A number of period newspapers in the
Alabama Archives yielded material: *Montgomery Weekly Mail,
Selma Times-Journal, Selma Press, Selma Times and Messenger,
Talladega Watchtower, Talladega Sun, Montgomery Weekly State
Journal,* and *Alabama Journal.* The Huntsville Public Library
has a nearly complete collection of the *Huntsville Advocate,* a
widely read Republican newspaper during Reconstruction.
The Cincinnati Historical Society in Cincinnati, Ohio, houses
a collection of the *Cincinnati Daily Times,* which reported on
the court of inquiry in Patona following the hangings.

The Birmingham Public Library provided an important
link to the story with the minute books of the Selma, Rome,
and Dalton Railroad from 1867 to 1874. Other information
about the railroad was also found in the New York Public

Library and the Franklin Delano Roosevelt Library in Hyde Park, New York.

Material from William Luke's Canadian experience came from several sources. The foremost was the United Church of Canada Archives at Victoria University, Toronto, Ontario, Canada. The archives became the repository of Luke's ministerial information after the Wesleyan Methodist church united with several other denominations in 1925. Documents from the Annesley United Church, Markdale, Ontario, and correspondence with Elsie Williams, Harold Cosens, and Wallace Littlejohns completed the Canadian research. Calhoun County circuit court records contained several depositions from Luke's family relative to a suit filed against Calhoun County.

## PUBLIC DOCUMENTS

Calhoun County circuit court records in Anniston document litigation by Luke's widow following the tragedy. Fanny Ann Luke sued Calhoun County in 1871 and 1874, and both trials were appealed to the Alabama State Supreme Court. The appeals were found in the Supreme Court records housed in the Alabama Archives in Montgomery. The investigation of the Klan problem in the South was published as *Report of the Joint Select Committee to Inquire into the Condition of Affairs in the Late Insurrectionary States* (Washington: Government Printing Office, 1872). The Alabama testimony was crucial to reconstructing the tragedy. The 1861 Canadian East Census and the *Ninth Census of the United States,* Calhoun County 1870, were used to develop background material.

## SECONDARY SOURCES

### Alabama

No one can venture into writing about a town in Alabama without the help of the classics in the state's history. Specialized material for Alabama was developed from the research work of various writers: Walter Jones, *Geological Survey of Alabama* (University, Ala.: Wetumpka Printing Co., 1933); Jesse Richardson, *Alabama Encyclopedia* (Northport, Ala.: American Southern Printing Co., 1965); Willis Brewer, *Alabama: Her History, Resources* (Montgomery: Barret and Brown, 1872); Saffold Berney, *Handbook of Alabama* (Birmingham: Roberts and Son, 1892); and Ethel Armes, *The Story of Coal and Iron in Alabama* (Cambridge: The University Press, 1910). These works provided the geographical and technical information for the period and the setting.

Glover Moore's *A Calhoun County, Alabama, Boy in the 1860's* (reprint, Jackson: University of Mississippi Press, 1978), and H. C. Nixon's *Lower Piedmont Country* (New York: Duell, Sloan and Pearce, 1946) were extremely valuable for locale description. E. Grace Jemison, *Historic Tales of Talladega* (Montgomery: Paragon Press, 1955), and E. C. Betts, *Historic Huntsville* (Birmingham: Southern University Press, 1920), provided handy guides for other towns important to the story.

One of the more helpful studies in Reconstruction Alabama was Sarah W. Wiggins, *The Scalawag in Alabama Politics, 1865–1881* (University, Ala.: University of Alabama Press, 1977). Other works by Wiggins consulted were Sarah W. Wiggins, "What Is a Scalawag?" *Alabama Review* 25 (January 1972), and "Alabama: Democratic Bulldozing and Republican Folly," in Otto H. Olsen, *Reconstruction and Redemption in the South* (Baton Rouge: Louisiana State University Press, 1980). Of equal importance was Loren Schweninger, "The American Missionary Association and Northern Philanthropy in Reconstruction Alabama," *Alabama Historical Quarterly* 32 (Fall and Winter 1970): 129–57. No research of this period in Alabama is complete without Walter L. Fleming, *The Reconstruction of the Seceded States* (Spartanburg: Reprint Co., 1978).

## The South

Any understanding of Reconstruction is difficult without a thorough study of the mass of research in the area. Among the classics are Paul Buck, *The Road to Reunion* (Boston: Little, Brown, 1937); Hodding Carter, *The Angry Scar* (Garden City: Doubleday, 1959); Allen Trelease, *White Terror* (New York: Harper & Row, 1971); Otto H. Olsen, *Reconstruction and Redemption in the South* (Baton Rouge: Louisiana State University Press, 1980), and John Hope Franklin, *Reconstruction after the Civil War* (Chicago: University of Chicago Press, 1969). The tragedy of Reconstruction was also set into a larger picture by Robert S. Henry, *The Story of Reconstruction* (New York: Grosset & Dunlap, 1938).

## OTHER SOURCES CONSULTED

Allen, James S. *Reconstruction: A Study in Democracy.* New York: International Publishers, 1937.

Beltz, Herman. *Reconstructing the Union: Theory and Policy during the Civil War.* Ithaca, N.Y.: Cornell University Press, 1969.

Brock, William R. *An American Crisis: Congress and Reconstruction, 1865–1867.* New York: Harper & Row, 1963.

Brodie, Fawn N. *Thaddeus Stevens, Scourge of the South.* New York: W. W. Norton Company, 1959.

Craven, Avery. *Reconstruction: The Ending of the Civil War.* New York: Holt, Rinehart and Winston, 1969.

Cruden, Robert. *The Negro in Reconstruction.* Englewood Cliffs, N.J.: Prentice-Hall, 1969.

Current, Richard N. *Old Thad Stevens: A Story of Ambition.* Madison, Wisc.: University of Wisconsin Press, 1942.

Daniels, Jonathan. *Prince of Carpetbaggers.* Philadelphia: J. B. Lippincott Company, 1958.

Davis, Susan Lawrence. *Authentic History of the Ku Klux Klan, 1865–1877.* New York: S. L. Davis, 1924.

Dawes, Anna L. *Charles Sumner.* New York: Dodd, Mead and Company, 1892.

Dulles, Foster Rhea. *The United States since 1865.* Ann Arbor: University of Michigan Press, 1959.

Dunning, William Archibald. *Essays on the Civil War and Reconstruction.* New York: Macmillan Company, 1898.

Fleming, Walter Lynwood. *Civil War and Reconstruction in Alabama.* New York: Columbia University Press, 1905.

———, ed. *Documentary History of Reconstruction.* 2 vols. New York: McGraw-Hill, 1966.

Herbert, Hilary A., et al. *Why the Solid South.* Baltimore: R. H. Woodward & Company, 1890.

Horn, Stanley F. *The Invisible Empire: The Story of the Ku Klux Klan, 1866–1871.* Boston: Little, Brown and Company, 1939.

McKitrick, Eric L. *Andrew Johnson and Reconstruction.* Chicago: University of Chicago Press, 1960.

Nash, Howard P., Jr. *Andrew Johnson: Congress and Reconstruction.* Rutherford, N.J.: Fairleigh Dickinson University Press, 1972.

Patrick, Rembert W. *The Reconstruction of the Nation.* New York: Oxford University Press, 1967.

Scott, Eben Greenough. *Reconstruction during the Civil War.* Reprint. New York: Negro University Press, 1969.

Sterling, Dorothy. *The Trouble They Seen.* Garden City: Doubleday & Company, 1976.

Stampp, Kenneth M. *The Era of Reconstruction, 1865–1877.* New York: Alfred A. Knopf, 1966.

Trelease, Allen W. *Reconstruction: The Great Experiment.* New York: Harper & Row, 1971.

Wish, Harvey, ed. *Reconstruction in the South.* New York: Farrar, Straus and Giroux, 1965.

Woodson, Carter G. *A Century of Negro Migration.* Washington: Association for the Study of Negro Life and History, 1918.

Woodward, C. Vann. *Reunion and Reaction.* New York: Anchor Books, Doubleday & Company, 1956.

# INDEX

# Index

# Index